EXPRESSIVE ARTS THERAPIES IN SCHOOLS

MMB MUSIC, INC.

CONTEMPORARY ARTS BUILDING
3526 WASHINGTON AVENUE
SAINT LOUIS, MISSOURI 63103-1019 USA
314 531-9635; 800 543-3771 (USA/Canada); Fax 314 531-8384
http://www.mmbmusic.com

ABOUT THE AUTHORS

Karen Frostig, M.Ed., A.T.R., L.M.H.C., is a registered art therapist and an adjunct faculty member at Lesley College's Expressive Therapies Program in Graduate School of Arts and Social Sciences, Massachusetts College of Art, and DeCordova Museum School. She is the former Program Coordinator of the Art Therapy Program at McLean Hospital and former Art Director of a private school for emotionally disturbed boys. Karen is also an art therapy supervisor in the Cambridge Public Schools, and holds a private practice in art therapy. Her paintings have been on exhibition throughout New England and New York and are in a number of private collections. Ms. Frostig has presented at various state and national conferences including the National Art Therapy Conference and her writing has been published in the Journal of the Art Therapy Association. She lives in Newton, Massachusetts with her husband and seven-year-old son.

Michele Essex, M.A., L.M.H.C., is the Assistant Director of Field Training and faculty member at Lesley College's Graduate School of Arts and Social Sciences in the Counseling and Psychology and Expressive Therapies Programs. She oversees the field training of over 500 graduate students and develops training collaborations between the college and community mental health centers, counseling agencies, schools, and hospitals. Ms. Essex developed an intraprofessional training model for integrating expressive arts therapies into the Cambridge Public Schools. She coauthored an article published in the Journal of the American Art Therapy Association and has presented at numerous state and national conferences. Ms. Essex is a licensed mental health counselor, certified school guidance counselor, and former Chairperson for the Massachusetts Board of Allied Mental Health. She currently lives in Laguna Beach, California with her partner and his eight-year-old daughter.

EXPRESSIVE ARTS THERAPIES IN SCHOOLS

A Supervision and Program Development Guide

By

KAREN FROSTIG

and

MICHELE ESSEX

With a Contribution by

Julianne Hertz

CHARLES C THOMAS · PUBLISHER, LTD.
Springfield · Illinois · U.S.A.

Published and Distributed Throughout the World by

CHARLES C THOMAS • PUBLISHER, LTD.
2600 South First Street
Springfield, Illinois 62794-9265

ISBN 0-398-06868-2

Library of Congress Catalog Card Number: 98-13491

With THOMAS BOOKS *careful attention is given to all details of manufacturing
and design. It is the Publisher's desire to present books that are satisfactory as to their
physical qualities and artistic possibilities and appropriate for their particular use.*
THOMAS BOOKS *will be true to those laws of quality that assure a good name
and good will.*

Printed in the United States of America
SM - R-3

Library of Congress Cataloging in Publication Data

Frostig, Karen
    Expressive arts therapies in schools : a supervision and program development
guide / by Karen Frostig and Michele Essex ; with a contribution by Julianne
Hertz.
       p.   cm.
    Includes bibliographical references.
    ISBN 0-398-06868-2 (pbk.)
    1. School children--Mental health services--United States.
    2. Art--Therapeutic use--United States. I. Title.
LB3430.F76   1998
371.7'13--dc21   98-13491
                                                   CIP

CONTRIBUTOR

Julianne Hertz is a registered art therapist and licensed mental health counselor who is currently working in a geropsychiatric partial program. She has worked in various settings with diverse populations, including persons with AIDS, adult psychiatric patients, trauma survivors, and emotionally disturbed behaviorally disordered children. Ms. Hertz is also an adjunct faculty member in the Expressive Therapy Program at Lesley College. Her professional credits include publication in the Journal of the Art Therapy Association and a presentation at the National Art Therapy Conference and at the University of Michigan School of Social Work. Julianne Hertz is a three-dimensional artist who has shown her mixed media sculpture in galleries throughout California. She currently works on a commission only basis out of her private studio. She maintains a private practice in Watertown, Massachusetts where she lives with her three birds.

*To the children of Cambridge Public Schools
and children in public schools everywhere
who deserve access to expressive arts therapies.*

PREFACE

The goal of this guide is to provide recommendations and guidelines to expressive arts therapists and educators who work in school settings as therapists, supervisors, supervisees, or graduate school expressive arts interns. *Expressive arts therapy* and *expressive arts therapist* as we refer to these terms throughout this guide are used to describe therapeutic disciplines and practitioners that incorporate one or more of the arts into their treatment modality, such as: art therapy, music therapy, dance/movement therapy, psychodrama therapy, or expressive arts therapy.

How to Best Use This Book

For expressive arts interns who wants to work within a school setting, reading this guide preplacement can aid in their assessment and selection of a site and/or supervisor. Reading this guide again at the start of a placement helps the intern orient to a new system, as well as assist them in developing a vision of how to work within a school. The guidelines help the intern plan an effective treatment program for the children in the school, as well as anticipate how the year might unfold according to the school calendar. Rereading the guidelines at the different phases of the training placement will clarify issues that may be magnified during those phases.

This guide can also be used as a resource guide for individuals who are interested in advocating and promoting the value of providing expressive arts therapies services in school settings. The Supervision and Program Development Guide suggests ideas for setting up or expanding an expressive arts therapy program in a school setting that can be further developed by expressive arts therapy supervisors and interns, program administrators, expressive arts therapy faculty from affiliating colleges, public school administrators, and school-based counselors. The guide systematically formulates program development for the various professionals engaged in designing an effective training program for expressive arts therapy interns, as well as an effective treatment program for children needing expressive arts therapy services in the public schools. As an instructive tool, this guide can help to clarify the purpose of expressive arts therapies within the school environment. It is important to emphasize here, that the guide is not intended to regulate the practice of expressive arts therapies in school settings. Rather, it is to provide structure and guidance, and to clarify expectations, so that the artistry of practicing expressive arts therapies is free to develop. Supervision is a self direct-ed process, entailing good communication and a willingness to learn and reflect upon experience. The guide supports that process.

The Supervision and Program Development Guide assists both supervisor and supervisee to have a better understanding and preparation for the super-visory relationship. This process ultimately helps to shape the professional development of both supervisee and supervisor. The guide is organized to provide readers with a practical and conceptual framework for school-based expressive arts therapies as well as a detailed supervision model and guide. It supplies supervisors and supervisees with a list of topics to help focus the supervision, maximizing the supervisee's learning through structure and orga-nization. The guide contains forms which help supervisors and supervisees conceptualize treatment. It provides strategies of approach and potential solutions to deep-seated systems problems. The guide includes various steps for independent program development between weekly supervision meetings and serves as a means to measure and mark weekly accomplishments.

In cases where this guide is being used by expressive arts interns and supervisees, the educative nature of it helps to lower anxiety levels, thereby allowing greater freedom to explore and investigate areas of vulnerability in their own processes of professional development. For supervisors this guide can serve to engender new approaches to supervision and further validate their professional role within the school. Supervisors and supervisees alike are certain to find the clear and concise case management forms and guide-lines contained within this guide to be assistance in the organization and mon-itoring of cases.

A Historical Context of Expressive Arts Therapies

Since antiquity, the healing powers of expressive art modalities have been recognized. For centuries, art, music, and movement have been used thera-peutically by many cultures in various situations. Beginning with the 1900s, the modalities have developed into specialized schools of psychotherapy.

From the experiences of WWII, a new awareness of the extent of mental illness developed in the U.S. which directly affected the development of expressive arts therapy. Men either rejected from military service or dis-charged with emotional difficulties numbered two million. After the war, rehabilitation of veterans with posttraumatic stress (shell shock) became a prevalent issue.

Psychoanalysis was the accepted treatment of the time. One to one ana-lytic therapy was found not effective in dealing with the veteran's problems. Nor was it an efficient solution to the numbers needing treatment. Along with other theories and approaches, expressive therapy was an efficient solution to the numbers needing treatment. Along with other theories and approaches, expressive arts therapy was developed as a way to facilitate rehabilitation through group work and time-limited treatment.

To offer the reader an historical context, what follows are extremely abbreviated narrative timelines of music, art, and dance/movement therapy.

Music

Documentation of music as therapy dates back to Egyptian times when priests/physicians often included chant therapies as part of medical practice. In Greece, the use of music for curing mental disorders reflected the belief that music could directly influence emotion and develop character. Both Aristotle and Plato wrote about the healing properties of music. Aristotle described the use of music for emotional catharsis and Plato described it as the medicine of the soul.

During the Renaissance, music was used as a remedy for what was then called "melancholy and madness." During that time, music was prescribed as preventative medicine for these and other physical illnesses.

In the United States, the use of music therapy began in educational institutions in 1832 when in Boston, the Perkins School for the Blind was founded by Dr. Samuel Gridley. Perkins integrated music into the curriculum at that time and music therapy continues to be an integral part of the program to this day.

In the 1940s the use of music therapy in the treatment of psychiatric disorders became more widespread. Many therapists, including the psychiatrist, Karl Meninger, began to advocate a holistic approach to treatment. It was at this time that music therapy became an accepted treatment modality in many hospitals.

Art

The first documentation of art as therapy dates back to the 14th century in the writings of Opicinius de Canastrius in which he describes how he used his artistic images to heal from illness. For many centuries, it appears that although the benefits of art were known, art and therapy developed separately. In the early 1900s, in Europe, documentation of the use of art in psychiatry appears.

Art and therapy were brought together in WWI by Carl Jung. Each morning, while a commandant of a prisoners of war camp in Switzerland, he would sketch mandalas in a notebook. He later wrote how these images described his "inner situation at the time" (Jung, 1961, p. 195), and how he could use the drawings to observe daily psychic changes (p. 196).

Hans Prinzhorn, a German psychiatrist, in the 1920s, collected over 5000 pieces of art done by patients in psychiatric institutions during the period from 1890–1920. This extensive compilation of work is available as *Artistry of the Mentally Ill.*

Art therapy coalesced into a field in the United States in the late 1940s and early 1950s through the work of Margaret Naumburg and Florence Cane. Naumburg was a psychoanalyst who focused on the use of image-making as an act of sublimation. Cane, an art educator, focused on what happens during image-making. Her work was based on the belief that the creative process of producing aesthetic objects is what is therapeutic. Since these sisters began their work, the development of art therapy has been influenced by various theories of psychotherapy, creating many approaches which utilize the tenets of each theory.

Dance/Movement

In dance therapy, movement interaction is used as the primary means for achieving therapeutic goals. Its roots date back to ancient times of tribal dances which were used to define individual or group identity, as expressions of celebration and crises, and in rituals of death and exorcism.

The development of dance as therapy is in part due to the revolutionary ways Isadora Duncan, and other pioneers of modern dance, changed the world of dance by breaking down the structure of classical ballet and creating dance as an expression of emotions in harmony with nature.

In 1942, Marion Chace was invited to begin dance therapy with patients at St. Elizabeth's hospital in Washington D.C. Her approach which stressed individuality of expression, is now known as Authentic Movement.

In the 1950s, Rudolf Laban, developed a system of analyzing and describing movement behavior according to the dynamic and spatial qualities of movement. This method allows the therapist to make diagnostic evaluations in movement terms. The observations are then used to help the dance therapist choose movement sequences most effective in achieving treatment goals.

Like the other expressive art modalities, theories of dance/movement have continued to develop and evolve since that time.

The Case for Providing Expressive Arts Therapies in School Settings

The focus on schools as a place to provide expressive arts therapies is an important one. These modalities of treatment frequently help to reach children who do not easily respond to traditional talk therapy. For anyone who has spent time working in schools, it has become increasingly clear that the severity of problems that children bring into school settings is rising dramatically. Violence, sexual abuse, suicide, substance abuse, poverty, and the decay of family and community structures are just some of the numerous issues affecting children today. While historically the function of schools was solely to educate children, more and more schools are becoming havens for children in distress. Schools are often the only safe, stable, and structured environment in a child's life.

In our current cultural climate schools are being expected to handle children who face very serious, complicated, challenging issues from home and social environments that make it difficult for them to focus and learn in the classroom setting. Schools and school professionals are being expected to do more with less money and fewer resources available to them.

Many public schools have been reluctant to house clinical services, preferring instead to refer children back to community mental health agencies for treatment. In the past, when children exhibited serious emotional or behavioral problems, they were sent to private therapeutic day schools or residential schools funded by their school district. With the decline of state and federal funds for education and the emphasis on an inclusion model of education public schools have begun to incorporate more school-based services.

School-based counseling including expressive arts therapies needs to become available in more schools across the nation. One compelling reason for this recommendation is that there is a large population of underserved children who never make it through the door of a community mental health center or a private practice office. Either a lack of money, resistance, fear, denial, or general disorganization could prevent a child from making an office visit at a particular time each week. The development of a trusting therapeutic relationship particularly for disenfranchised or at-risk children or those with histories of trauma requires more than offering a "safe space" to talk and the assurance of confidentiality. Children need to "check out" their therapists. They need to get a sense of who their therapists are before they learn to trust them. The visibility and accessibility of school-based counselors facilitates the formation of therapeutic alliances which are frequently more successful than those in clinics or private practice therapy where a child usually sees a therapist only once a week.

Providing expressive arts therapies within school settings requires that schools either hire or contract with expressive arts therapists to deliver services in schools. Frequently on- or off-site expressive arts therapists also provide supervision to expressive arts interns or school-based therapists. The importance of supervision is therefore critical in providing professional guidance, development, and leadership for supervisees.

K.F.
M.E.

ACKNOWLEDGMENTS

There are numerous individuals deserving of thanks who contributed in various ways to this publication. The establishment of the original collaboration between Lesley College and Cambridge Public Schools included the support and efforts of Mary Ann Gawelek, former Dean of the Counseling and Psychology Programs, Ellen Willard, Associate Director of Bureau of Pupil Services at Cambridge Public Schools, and Russ Lyman, Director of the Cambridge Youth Guidance Center. This collaboration would not have been possible without the willingness of Cambridge school counselors to serve as "on-site" supervisors. The combined efforts of all who participated in this collaboration created the milieu out of which this guide emerged.

Julianne Hertz, an art therapy supervisor in the collaborative, joined us as a contributing editor, authoring *Historical Context of Expressive, Art, Music Dance/Movement Therapies*. Her input, at many different junctures, greatly enhanced the development of this guide.

Lesley's expressive arts therapy students made tremendous contributions, not only to the children with whom they worked, but also to the ongoing improvement of this collaborative training model. Although many originally viewed this as "merely" an expressive arts therapy training experience, they soon discovered that their participation in this pilot program was a pioneering effort to establish expressive arts therapy in the public schools. Art therapy intern, Laurie Anderson, is responsible for creating the Weekly Log in the Appendices.

Special thanks to the Field Training Office for the clerical, administrative, and organizational support lent to this project. Lesley faculty members who made contributions include Terri Halperin-Eaton, dance/movement therapist and Michele Forinash, music therapist, who contributed dance and music terminology to the thesaurus. Susan Spaniol, art therapy faculty member, provided structural and ethical guidance for our 1997 Cambridge City Hall exhibition of Cambridge Public School children's art and performance work. Other Lesley faculty that supported our efforts include: Julia Byers, Program Director of Expressive Therapies, Mariagnese Cattaneo, Director of Field Training and Martha McKenna, Dean of the Graduate School of Arts and Social Sciences. Special gratitude goes to the artists who contributed their work and Brent Levinson, whose support and interest in this book was realized by his willingness to read and provide feedback to the many drafts that preceded the final printing of this book.

TERMINOLOGY

Below is a list of frequently-used terms throughout this guide.

Expressive Arts Therapy: A term used to describe all therapeutic disciplines that incorporate the arts into their treatment modality, such as: art therapy, music therapy, dance therapy, psychodrama therapy, and expressive therapy. This term, like "creative arts therapies" is used when referring to all of the disciplines using the arts as a vehicle of expression.

Expressive Arts Therapist: A term used to describe a clinician that incorporates one or more of the expressive arts modalities (art therapy, music therapy, psychodrama therapy, drama therapy, or expressive therapy) into their practice.

Expressive Arts Products and Processes: (1) Expressive Arts Products is a term that refers to the creative outcome of an expressive arts therapy experience, resulting in a tangible object, such as: art work (paintings, drawings, and sculptures), videos (tapes of dance or performance pieces), and cassettes (tapes of music, or poetry readings). The products are reflective of the different arts modalities: art, music, dance, drama, and expressive, and can emerge from individual work or group work. (2) Expressive Arts Processes is a term that refers to a variety of arts experiences, representative of all of the arts modalities, that does not necessarily culminate in a final arts product.

Supervisee: Refers to any professional within the school system (for example: an expressive arts therapist in training, a credentialed expressive arts therapist, a special education specialist, an art educator, a guidance counselor, a clinical psychologist, an occupational therapist, or a social worker), conducting expressive arts therapy services with children, under the guidance of a credentialed, supervising expressive arts therapist.

Intern: A term used to refer to a graduate school trainee, contracted to work in the schools as an expressive arts therapist in training, for a year's placement. An intern can be in their first, second, or third year of training; generally enrolled in a graduate school program linked to expressive arts therapy or a related discipline.

Supervisor: Refers to any credentialed clinician who oversees the work of the supervisee or intern.

At-Risk Youth: A term used to identify children and adolescents, prone to academic failure due to a variety of "risk factors," that include: emotional disturbance and/or social adjustment problems, which can be further compounded by family issues of neglect, violence, and/or poverty.

CONTENTS

		Page
Preface		ix
Terminology		xv
Chapter		
1.	EXPRESSIVE ARTS THERAPIES IN SCHOOL SETTINGS	3
	Definition of On-Site and Off-Site Supervision	4
	Contract Supervision	4
	Definition of Supervisor/Supervisee Roles	4
	Expressive Arts Therapies Supervisor	4
	School-Based Counselor Supervisor	6
	Supervisees	6
	Learning Objectives and Responsibilities	7
	Learning Objectives	7
	Responsibilities (Weekly)	8
	Confidentiality in School Settings	8
	Ethical Guidelines	9
	The School Calendar	9
	For the Children	9
	For the Expressive Arts Intern	9
	For the Supervisor	10
	Bringing Closure to the Supervisee/Supervisor Relationship	12
	School Culture: Multiculturalism and Expressive Arts Therapies	12
	Presenting Issues of Children Referred for School-Based Expressive Arts Therapies	13
	Shared Goals of Expressive Arts Therapies and Education	15
2.	SUPERVISION GUIDELINES	19
	What is Supervision?	19
	Supervision Guidelines	20
	Guidelines for the Supervisee	20
	Guidelines for Supervisors	25
	Discussing Difficult Topics in Supervision	28
3.	CASE MANAGEMENT GUIDELINES	31
	Case Management and Structural Guidelines	31
	Description of Case Management Forms	31

	Weekly Log	31
	Referral Form	31
	Process Note	32
	Group Protocol	32
	Mini-Case Presentation Format	32
	Release Form	32
	Termination Report	33
4.	COLLABORATION AND COMMUNICATION GUIDELINES	35
	Establishing Consistent School-Wide and System-Wide Policies	35
	Guidelines for Meetings with Families of Children Receiving Expressive Arts Therapies Services	35
	Guidelines for Handling Discipline	36
	Guidelines for Identifying and Reporting Suspected Abuse	37
	Guidelines for Exhibiting Expressive Arts Products	37
5.	OBSERVATIONS AND EVALUATION: Process and Procedures	43
	Observations	43
	Observation Guidelines	43
	Observations and Feedback	45
	Evaluations	46
	Difficult Evaluations	46
	Conditions Warranting Termination of an Intern's Contract	47
6.	PROFESSIONAL DEVELOPMENT	49
	Credentialing and Licensing	49
	Continued Professional Development as a Clinician	49
	Continuing Education	49
	Membership in Professional Associations	50
	Peer Supervision Groups	51
	Subscriptions to Professional Journals	51
	Continued Professional Development Within One's Modality	51
7.	GUIDELINES FOR INTRODUCING AND PROMOTING EXPRESSIVE ARTS THERAPIES IN SCHOOL SETTINGS	55
	Recommendations for Contacting Schools to Explore Consulting, Employment or Training Opportunities in Expressive Arts Therapies	55
	Linking up with a Graduate School of Art, Dance, Music, or Expressive Arts Therapies if One is Located in Your Area	55
	Becoming Employed by Public School Systems	55
	Getting into a School System When You Don't Have the Required Credentials	56
	Inclusion Programs	56

Developing After-Hours School-Based Expressive Arts
    Therapies Programs   56
Importance of Professional Presentation   56
Writing a Proposal to Promote the Addition of Expressive Arts
    Therapies Services to Schools and Other Settings   57
Developing a Format for Expressive Arts Therapies
    In-Service Presentation for Staff   57
Useful Questions to Ask at Informational or Site Interviews   58
Year in Review Program Evaluation   59
End-of-Year Program Review and Evaluation   60
8.   CONCLUSION   63
Appendix A. Case Management Forms   65
Appendix B. Evaluation Forms   89
Appendix C. Additional Resources   103

EXPRESSIVE ARTS THERAPIES
IN SCHOOLS

Figure 1: K. L., age 6.

Chapter 1

EXPRESSIVE ARTS THERAPIES
IN SCHOOL SETTINGS

Although there is a significant body of literature on expressive arts therapies within schools, much of it represents work which takes place in specialized settings. There is little in the literature which addresses the development of the role of expressive therapies in public schools, the integration of the expressive arts into the main school program, and the collaboration among members of an interdisciplinary staff. Some articles address the use of art and expressive therapies with children who, as a result of emotional difficulties, have been referred through the school system to a separate treatment setting for individual or group therapy (Zeiger, 1994; Steinhardt, 1993). In the current climate of dwindling social service resources, referral to inpatient treatment, residential facilities, and mental health agencies has become increasingly difficult. Only those children in the most acute distress can, usually after a prolonged time period, receive time-limited services at these facilities. The result is that greater numbers of more disturbed children remain in the classrooms of the public schools. The expressive arts therapist must explore how these factors shape and define the clinical expressive work to be accomplished in the schools.

The inclusion of expressive arts therapies in school settings may be increasing, however, these services are not necessarily provided by an expressive arts therapist employed within the school system. Schools sometimes augment their services by hiring expressive arts therapists as consultants or by providing internship training experiences for expressive arts interns. An intraprofessional collaborative approach to working with children in school systems is on the increase and as such requires that the roles and definitions of these individuals be clearly articulated.

The training model described below provides clarifying definitions, learning objectives, and training responsibilities to assist those interested in working collaboratively to provide expressive arts therapies in school settings. The following individuals can benefit from utilizing an intraprofessional model of training and supervision in their work in schools:

- Therapists
- Educators

- Supervisors (on-site or off-site)
- Supervisees
- Expressive Arts Interns

Definition of On-Site and Off-Site Supervision

The definition of an on-site supervisor is simply an individual who is primarily based in the school and is usually employed by the school system. Off-site supervisors are generally contracted by either expressive arts therapists or expressive arts interns when there is no expressive arts supervisor based in the school.

Contract Supervision

Contract expressive arts therapies supervisors provide supervision pro bono or for a fee that is paid for by the supervisee or the school system. A contract supervisor should have a written agreement with the supervisee and school regarding the supervision to be provided. A copy of the written agreement with a contract supervisor should be provided to and maintained on file by appropriate personnel at the school (generally the supervisee's assigned supervisor). Periodic evaluations of the supervisee should be completed by the contract supervisor and reviewed and maintained on file by appropriate personnel at the school.

In cases where supervision is provided by off-site supervisors, it is essential that an on-site supervisor is also available to the supervisee. The on-site supervisor when an expressive arts therapist is not employed by the school is generally a school-based counselor such as a school guidance counselor, school adjustment counselor, or school psychologist.

Definition of Supervisor/Supervisee Roles

The following definitions provide some guidelines and expectations for individuals in the role of expressive arts therapies supervisor, school-based counselor supervisor or supervisee.

Expressive Arts Therapies Supervisor

The expressive arts therapies supervisor is responsible for providing expressive arts therapies supervision for supervisees for preferably one hour weekly. S/he models, mentors, and instructs supervisees on expressive arts therapies assessment tools, techniques, and modalities appropriate for working with children in a school setting. Supervisors attend to the development of supervisees and help to consolidate his/her professional identity as an expressive arts therapist. When the expressive arts therapies supervisor is off-site, s/he tries to hold supervision sessions at the school site, or, when that is not possible, attempts to make site visits on a regular basis to observe supervisees utilizing expressive arts therapies with children. The expressive arts therapies supervisor discusses in periodic evaluation meetings with supervisees areas of growth, progress, and challenges.

The expressive arts therapies supervisor helps supervisees translate expressive arts therapies theory into practice, following the continuum from a broad understanding to individual applications for specific children. This includes providing knowledge about psychosocial and artistic developmental stages. The supervisor works with the supervisee to identify diagnostic information from which to formulate expressive arts therapies treatment plans.

One premise of expressive arts therapies is that the image represents significant metaphors, which when properly understood, provide insight into the developmental, affective and social world of the student. The expressive arts therapies supervisor teaches clinical skills by developing a supervisee's understanding of this expressive image. S/he helps the supervisee internalize the process of using symbols to further the clinical work and to gain access to the child's interior experience. It is within this context that the supervisor brings the expressive modalities into supervision. The expressive arts therapies supervisor teaches the supervisee to use his/her chosen modality to learn more about the child's process as well as the supervisee's reactions as an expressive arts therapist.

The expressive process enhances children's normative developmental patterns and communication skills. It is also the role of the expressive arts therapies supervisor to teach the supervisee how to use expressive arts therapies to develop these patterns and skills; resulting in improvement in the child's functional capacity in the classroom and at home.

Throughout the training year, the expressive arts therapies supervisor teaches the supervisee to use his/her experience to gain a greater understanding of the role of expressive arts therapies in the schools. In the role of advocate, the expressive arts therapies supervisor provides organizational assistance and support to assure that the supervisee has the needed resources to work effectively within the system. Examples include: mailboxes, office space, adequate supply budgets.

The expressive arts therapies supervisor explains to supervisees ways to maximize their training experience and presence in the schools. This includes initiating contact with educators and specialists to attract and gain referrals. Supervisees are encouraged to promote expressive arts therapies through conversations with school personnel, presentation of in-services, and through a professional comportment. The supervisor must emphasize how important this initial phase is to set the tone for a productive and successful year.

The supervisor initially serves as a liaison between the supervisee and the system to ensure that the framework of program development gets put in place. The supervisor facilitates the flow of referrals until the supervisee reaches appropriate clinical competencies and communication skills. The supervisor ensures that the supervisee maintains a diversified caseload (diagnosis, culture, individual, group). Once the supervisee's caseload is adequate, the supervisor helps develop individual treatment plans and ideas for groups, based on the needs of students referred for treatment, linking expressive arts therapies goals to educational goals.

School-Based Counselor Supervisor

Each supervisee should be assigned a school-based counselor who is designated as the supervisee's primary on-site supervisor when an expressive arts therapies supervisor is not employed within the school. The primary supervisor provides direction for the supervisee's work (assigns cases and groups, is the liaison to the families, helps with scheduling of space, supplies, etc.). The role of the school-based counselor is generally to create a supportive environment within the school where the skills and resources necessary for problem-solving and conflict resolution are accessible to all.

School-based counselors usually work with children, staff, and families to achieve a broad base of commonly shared knowledge concerning the school climate, establishment of classroom rules and norms, and social skills development. The understanding and appreciation of different family configurations and cultural diversity is significantly stressed within the role functioning of the school counselor.

The school-based counselor should guide, mentor, support, and advocate for supervisees to become skilled at functioning as counselors within the system. S/he should provide a minimum of one hour of weekly supervision and discuss in periodic evaluation meetings with supervisees areas of growth, progress, and challenges.

Supervisees

Supervisees are expected to work with school personnel in developing a responsive expressive arts therapies program to service the school's population of "at-risk" youth as well as individual referrals of special needs children. Supervisees are expected to join educators in a unified commitment toward the cognitive, emotional, social, and creative development of children by establishing clear art and expressive arts therapies objectives that interact with educational goals. Supervisees contract a weekly schedule that meets program requirements and are expected to fulfill their responsibilities with consistency, dependability, and accountability. Keeping of ethical standards of confidentiality, signing release forms, maintaining student portfolios, documenting treatment, and reporting suspected abuse serve to protect the children in treatment and define the context of the work.

Learning Objectives and Responsibilities

The following is a sample of learning objectives and responsibilities that can assist both supervisees and supervisors to formulate goals and workload expectations within a training program or an employment situation. This model can be adapted and expanded upon by expressive arts therapists and expressive arts interns to best meet their professional goals and the needs of their role within the school setting.

Learning Objectives

- Develop a multicultural perspective in utilizing expressive arts therapies with children
- Develop ability to work with children and/or adolescents in individual and group counseling
- Learn to listen and respond appropriately to racial, sexual, social, and ethnic differences
- Develop an understanding of how to effectively utilize the intraprofessional relationships
- Strengthen ability to set clear, supportive limits, and follow through on limit setting
- Learn interview and assessment techniques
- Learn how to write and implement treatment plans geared for the academic setting
- Utilization of process recording notes
- Develop a working relationship with staff members, and parents, and outside professionals
- Gain an understanding of how expressive arts therapies may enhance a child's school experience
- Develop an awareness of transference and countertransference issues
- Establish a professional identity as expressive arts therapist working within a school setting

Responsibilities (Weekly)

- 2-5 hours individual counseling
- 3-4 hours group work (includes 1 hour planning and 30 minutes group process time)
- 3 hours milieu work
- 1 hour crisis intervention
- 1 hour case management
- 1 hour consultation with teachers, parents, school staff
- 1 hour meeting on "Students at Risk"
- 1 hour meeting on referred students with special needs
- 1 hour administrative work
- 1 hour weekly individual supervision with an expressive arts therapist
- 1 hour weekly individual supervision with school counselor (when expressive arts therapies supervisor is off-site)

Confidentiality in School Settings

Confidentiality in school settings has it's own unique set of challenges given the extended system of professionals who work with the child and family. Confidentiality is generally regarded as an absolute. Interpreted from the perspective of working with children, confidentially is a professional ethic that would protect the child from unauthorized disclosures by the expressive arts therapist without consent of the child. Confidentiality is a contract between the expressive arts therapist and the child with explicit understanding that nothing about the child will be revealed except under conditions agreed to by the child. However, there are ethical and legal exceptions that require professionals to be aware that confidentiality in the therapeutic relationship is limited. This is particularly true when working with children. There are conditions under which confidentiality should be broken. These conditions include instances when the child presents a serious and imminent danger to him/herself or others or when there is suspected child abuse or neglect.

Expressive arts therapists are also advised to be aware of the privileged communication laws in the state in which they are practicing. Privileged communication is a right granted by law to certain professionals not to testify in court in regards to information confidential in nature that was obtained within the counseling relationship. Privileged communication laws are interpreted strictly by the courts. Expressive arts therapists are advised to know how the exact word of the law is interpreted in the state in which they practice. For example, some states extend privilege communication to school-based counselors while others do not.

Ethical Guidelines

In the field of expressive arts therapies, as in all professions, there are guidelines which mandate that practitioners behave in both ethical and legal ways. It is important that expressive arts therapists know the ethical guidelines set forth in their professional association's code of ethics. In addition, it is strongly recommended that expressive arts therapist be well-informed about the code of ethics adhered to by state licensing boards and/or national counseling associations that govern standards in counseling in the state in which they practice. In general, there is much consensus among the ethical codes of the various associations.

The School Calendar

The school setting has a particular calendar that helps to shape certain patterns within a nine month time-frame. Part of the task of supervision is to help expressive arts interns or newly hired school-based expressive arts therapists anticipate the ebbs and flows of the treatment according to the school calendar.

For the Children

September marks the end of summer and the return to academic life, structure, classroom routines and expectations, and focused peer interactions. Holiday fever begins by mid-October and continues through January. December vacation is riddled with hopes and dreams, real-life limitations, and harsh disappointments. Anxiety about unstructured time, unstable home lives, loss of the professional support children have begun to trust, and on an unconscious level, fear of decompensation, all are heightened around the December holidays.

The period of late winter to early spring marks a time of stabilization, work, and growth. The termination process begins with April vacation and unfolds over the final two months of school. Accomplishments, increased sunshine, heartfelt yearnings, and sadness can characterize this period of time, as children prepare to say good-bye to a network of caring and attentive adults.

The school-based calendar progression for children parallels the unfolding of the intern's academic calendar.

For the Expressive Arts Intern

From September through October, the intern is in the adjustment phase. S/he is adjusting to a new school, new professors, new circle of students or peers, and sometimes, even a new city and set of roommates.

Thanksgiving signals a brief return to home for the holidays or, if the distance is too great, a longing for home.

The December holidays on campus signal an increase in workload for trainees and results in stress levels which parallel the children's experience in the public schools. End-of-semester papers are due, along with the financial pressures of registering for spring semester classes. Childhood memories mixed up with new discoveries about oneself converge at the close of an emotional, introspective stretch of classes. Self-doubts may emerge about the choice of expressive arts therapies as a profession.

January through April is defined by a surge of competency. Interns come to understand the work and to interact effectively with a range of school-based educators and specialists. They develop real connections to children. They become more flexible in their use of expressive arts therapies and are clearer about clinical goals, limit setting, and creative experimentation and expression.

The end of the year is bittersweet for interns. Again, papers are due, but this time it is easier than the first round. Interns are better able to anticipate the work, to know what is expected, and to generally feel more confident and competent. They also anticipate the summer reprieve from the ongoing pressures of being a student.

The manner in which the intern goes about ending the therapeutic relationship with children is understood from a training perspective, as a measure of the supervisee's clinical expertise. Often these good-byes are the first real good-byes of their lives. For the trainee, the challenge of clinical proficiency is to both experience the feelings as well as to observe them, so as to facilitate a meaningful experience of saying good-bye. Good weather tempers the ambivalence of saying good-bye. The metaphor of "the season of growth" can be incorporated into the framework of ending. The second year promises vitality and hope, softening the loss of relationships with the many children to whom attachments have been formed.

The year thus concludes with the spirit of earned exhilaration, based on the intern's clarification of his or her purpose and identification as an expressive arts therapist. Patterns in supervision also echo the school calendar.

For the Supervisor

Beginnings, middles, and ends occur simultaneously for children, teachers, and support staff, including expressive arts therapies supervisees and their supervisors. It is the responsibility of the supervisor to contextualize the learning process for the supervisee within this calendar progression. The calendar formulation can help a supervisee and his/her supervisor prepare for certain stressful periods within the whole system.

Supervisors must be particularly available in the first few months of the year, helping to establish the intern in his or her new role as an expressive arts therapy trainee. Typically in this early orientation phase of supervision, there are extra meetings, phone check-ins, and introductions. Meetings are facilitated between the intern and teachers, school specialists, and administrators. Groups may be co-led, and arrangements be made for the intern to observe expressive arts therapy groups in progress. The extra effort that the supervisor puts into these early months is made in good faith, with the belief that it will be time-limited. The intern will recirculate energy back into the system, as s/he gains confidence and independence in the new role.

By December, the supervisor intuitively pulls back. The intern is expected to begin to work more independently, carrying a full caseload. As the supervisor shifts from full availability to restricted availability, s/he may experience unspoken confusion or resentment on the part of the intern, triggering countertransference feelings, including guilt, doubt, entitlement, and anger. In turn, the intern may replace early idealization of his or her supervisor with a more realistic appraisal of their supervisor's strengths and weaknesses. The emotional climate between supervisor and supervisee may be conflicted and distrustful. Both evaluate each other's performance and prepare for the next stretch of collaboration, which is "developmentally" different from the first.

The index of the intern's surge of competency in the time of January through April must be appropriately met by the supervisor's ability to trust in the competency of the intern and to "let go." This process enables the intern to "find his or her way" and gain his or her authentic voice as a therapist in training. This can be a very rich and gratifying phase of supervision, where the learning curve of the intern arches to its fullest potential.

Termination is the focus of the last two months. Supervisors clarify the process of saying "good-bye" by valuing its importance and repeatedly reminding the intern of its imminence. Good-byes trigger a sense of loss for children, particularly those who have already suffered many significant losses in life. For these children, the end of the therapeutic relationship becomes an opportunity to rework an earlier good-bye through grieving, healing and growing. The emotional complexity of the process deepens the intern's clinical understanding of work with children. The supervisor models sitting with the supervisee, processing the mix of resistance and yearning, the wish to hold on as well as to let go of the children. The supervisor decodes the parallel feelings expressed by the children in a startling array of behaviors, so that the intern comes to appreciate the child's immense and fragile dependency, trust, and love for the intern. This process generates poignant, vulnerable, and tender moments between supervisor and supervisee. The manner in which the supervisor facilitates this unique phase of the work sets in motion the final phase of the supervisory relationship, the year is framed and evaluated by both the supervisor and supervisee.

Evaluation and reflection go hand in hand. In this final phase, the year is often relived. Each treatment relationship is reviewed, as is each child's struggle to grow, to gain social competencies, to integrate a range of affect. Each child settles into a role as learner, explores creative self-expression, and meets the intern in the therapeutic process. This parallel process becomes a metaphor of the intern's own capacity to meet each child, to care, to problem-solve, to assist, and to be fully present as listener and healer. The child's growth affirms the intern's belief in his or her own process of development.

Bringing Closure to the Supervisee/Supervisor Relationship

At the close of the school calendar year, the supervisory relationship comes to an end. Terminating the supervisee/supervisor occurs after the intern has completed all school-based responsibilities and submitted appropriate paperwork (termination summaries and supervision evaluations). Spontaneous gift-making, symbolically representing the supervisory relationship, is sometimes exchanged between supervisee and supervisor. An art experience can sometimes be developed to ritualize the final meeting.

School Culture: Multiculturalism and Expressive Arts Therapies

Multicultural counseling can be defined as any therapeutic relationship in which the therapist and client differ with respect to values, lifestyle, and cultural background. In the case of school-based counseling in urban settings, where most expressive arts therapists are white and female, an awareness of multiculturalism is essential in their work with children of different racial, socioeconomic and ethnic backgrounds. Multiculturalism in schools has evolved out of an awareness and appreciation of difference. Schools have become the most vibrant symbol of the pluralistic society in which we live. Multiculturalism follows the inclusive model in education, ensuring that marginalized groups are fully represented, creating an atmosphere of social equality and respect.

Multiculturalism finds a comfortable habitat in expressive arts therapies. While multiculturalism seeks to affirm every individual, eliminate stereotypes, and create dialogue, expressive arts therapy encourages individual voice, appreciates multiple perspectives, and values authenticity. Multiculturalism builds community; expressive arts therapy builds bridges between people. Both honor the individual within the group; both seek to reduce isolation, creating empathic links between people.

Multiculturalism includes all points of view as valid. Expressive arts therapy values group process, reflecting on how people affect each other with words, gestures, and actions. Both promote a democratic exchange.

Multiculturalism enjoys the artistic expression of many different cultures.

Expressive arts therapy encourages personal expression, consistent with one's personal and cultural sense of self. Multiculturalism is alive with spirit and hope; expressive arts therapy heals the spirit and restores wholeness. Both thrive in schools, providing enrichment and renewal.

Presenting Issues of Children Referred For School-Based Expressive Arts Therapies

The referral of children to school-based services is on the increase throughout our nation's public schools. One main reason for this is the inclusion mandate in most states to meet the needs of children with special needs, as well as more "at-risk" children who exhibit severe emotional difficulties and problem behaviors, within the classroom setting. In order to fulfill this mandate, public schools are needing to provide adjunctive treatment and services that enable children to function in the school environment.

The following list provides examples of specific situations or circumstances that may increase a child's vulnerability to risk factors: Some of these issues, in isolation, would not necessarily result in a referral to an expressive arts therapist. Referral for treatment generally only occurs if the child exhibits problematic behavior.

Although many of these issues cut across economic and racial lines, financial stability may offer some protection to children by creating a pseudosecure environment and by providing additional resources and experiences to offset some of the losses and traumas that are included in this list. It is important to note, however, that the *protection* or *buffer* afforded to children from more privileged socioeconomic backgrounds does not preclude their need for treatment.

A. Serious emotional or traumatic experience associated with nonschool environment

- Foster care
- Living in shelters
- Parent or close relative in jail
- Parent or close relative as a victim of violence
- Extreme poverty
- Adoption of an older child
- Recent immigration from a country with social, political, and economic upheaval
- Children of parents with major mental illness
- Children of a battered parent
- Children of parents frequently unemployed
- Trauma related to abduction or attempted abductions
- Trauma related to physical, sexual or verbal abuse

- Intergenerational incest
- Children witnessing violence in the neighborhood, in the home
- History of delinquency, theft, destruction of public property, arson
- Forced to participate in illegal activities, i.e. drug trafficking

B. Family factors that may increase vulnerability*

- Single parent families
- Divorced families
- Adoptive families
- Multiple moves and changes in schools
- Living with a grandmother or a relative other than parents
- Children of parents with frequent unemployment
- Children of a parent who gambles
- Children in the midst of a messy custody battle
- Absentee parents
- Absence of any routine "family time"
- Over achieving, critical parents placing unrealistic expectations on the child
- Latchkey kids
- Substance abuse

C. Behavior problems manifested in school

- Attention deficit disorders compounded by hyperactivity, on ritalin
- Repeated suspensions
- Bringing weapons to school
- Repeated incidents of stealing, cheating, lying
- Threatening teachers or other children
- Bullying behaviors
- Violent with classmates
- Truancy
- Provocative dressing
- Excessive obscene language
- Frequent angry and hateful displays of racism, sexism, classism
- Scapegoated by peers or teachers
- Frequent requests to see the nurse, somatization
- Learning disability
- Gifted

D. Other observable manifestations of behavior

- Attachment disorders

---

* Although these kinds of families may be at greater statistical risk, many will nevertheless thrive and function well.

- Developmental delays
- Eating disorder
- Frequent nightmares
- Stuttering
- Bedwetting
- Withdrawal
- Age inappropriate sexualized behaviors
- Violent with siblings, family members
- Animal torture
- Substance abuse
- Highly accident prone
- Suicidal
- Immature
- Guilt-ridden
- Excessive hand washing
- Secretive behaviors
- Anxious
- Always trying to please the adults
- Parentified child, family caretaker
- Promiscuous behavior, teenage pregnancy
- Rigid

E. Other risk factors

- Small size for age
- Obesity
- Held back a grade
- Children with AIDS or parents with AIDS
- Children living in unsafe neighborhoods, drug trafficking or random acts of violence
- Absence of a caring community
- Tight rigid family schedules that promote stress and decrease opportunities for play with other children
- Long-term exposure to violent or sexual programs on television

Shared Goals of Expressive Arts Therapies and Education

Many expressive arts therapies goals are compatible with educational goals. In the largest sense, both disciplines serve to further children's cognitive, social, and emotional development. Areas of overlap include the development of:

- Task Competencies

- Improved Interpersonal Skills
- Improved Motivation
- Sense of Discovery
- Risk Taking
- Creativity
- Release of Tension
- Improved Ability to Cope With Stress
- Self-Awareness Through Self-Expression
- Self-Esteem and Self-Confidence Through Mastery
- Self-Control Through Sublimation
- Group Cooperation Through Collaboration of Ideas
- Communication Skills
- Organizational Skills
- Problem-Solving Skills
- Aesthetic Sensibilities
- Spontaneity and Experimentation
- Integration of Experience

Identifying these goals serves the role of expressive arts therapies in schools by:

1. Reducing suspicious attitudes from both educators and parents about what expressive arts therapies actually does;
2. Placing expressive arts therapists in alliance with educators;
3. Delineating how expressive arts therapies can assist in improving a child's classroom behaviors;
4. Clarifying how expressive arts therapists contribute information as front-line workers, identifying issues and conflicts that interfere with school performance;
5. Informing expressive arts therapists about the direction and the content of their work with children;
6. Enabling expressive arts therapists to formulate treatment plans and strategies that will support children's ability to achieve these goals.

Figure 2: Terrill Becker, 1997, Art Therapy Intern.

Chapter 2

SUPERVISION GUIDELINES

What Is Supervision?

Supervision is a responsibility and commitment to supporting the growth of another. Supervision is a self-directed process, entailing good communication and a willingness by both parties to learn and reflect upon their experience. A good supervisor not only listens to what is being said, but also, to what is *not* being said. Ideally, supervision unfolds at its own pace, paralleling a nondirective treatment model. Two people sit together and discover the content of the work between them (e.g. the children, the art work, the system, and the supervisory relationship). The provision of support and direction occurs within the context of developing a clinical understanding of issues and goals.

In addition, supervisors serve as potential role models, providing guidance and direction, inspiring interns to reach their fullest potential as clinicians in training. The supervisor supports individual development of the supervisee and does not create an artificial timetable of what and when things should happen. A supervisor can also serve as a type of visionary, holding an image of how expressive arts therapy best works within a school setting and how a supervisee is expected to perform in their role. A good supervisor also affirms the supervisee's ability to initiate new ideas and put these ideas into practice.

> Each student intern requires an individual approach within the context of her characterological orientation. One may view supervision as a feeding, i.e., emotional nourishment that will ease the growth process. Another wants to use the power of the supervisor through submission and conquest. Still another may set up competitive situations and test out his or her mettle against the supposed superior authority. Fears regarding exposure often enter into the relationship and a need to be invulnerable may exist. The complexity of the attitudes seems as broad as any found in the therapeutic encounter. The underlying principle, therefore, is that each student attempts to utilize supervision to maximize his or her autonomous development. His or her resistances to learning and changing are recognized and respected. A sense of support and nonjudgement would seem to be the ideal atmosphere for such a relationship to flourish. The student's goal in supervision is toward developing a personal therapeutic style consistent with his or her own growth, rather than mimicking or idealizing a role model set forth by his or her own supervisor. Without an

effective and open dialogue with a supervisor, a student will be missing a most enriching part of his or her entire learning process.

(Robbins, 1994, p. 20)

Supervision Guidelines

The goal of supervision is to provide clinical training in expressive arts therapies by promoting confidence, competence, and professionalism. Supervision should be clinically focused, emphasizing the development of therapeutic skills in expressive arts therapies. It is recommended that supervision be used efficiently to cover the broad range of issues that arise in school-based counseling.

Establishing good communication and a genuine relationship will further the learning process between the supervisor and the supervisees. Items covered in these guidelines are recommended discussion during supervision. Although many of the guidelines are shared, the categories have been divided into responsibilities of supervisee and responsibilities of the supervisor. Supervision is an active process. It is up to the supervisee to take initiative throughout the year to insure a productive use of the supervisory process. It is up to the supervisor to guide this process to help maximize the supervisee's learning experience.

Guidelines for the Supervisee

I. Scheduling Meeting Times
    A. Ideally, supervision should be one hour per week. In many schools this is not possible because of the school schedule, therefore, having the flexibility to meet in scheduled time blocks is also acceptable. For example, two 1/2 hour meeting times.
    B. Reschedule canceled meetings.
    C. Request supervision coverage when a supervisor is on vacation or out sick over extended time.

II. Preparation for Supervision
    A. Be organized in presenting various problems or accomplishments of the week. Do not overlook identifying areas of success or assume that the supervisor will already be informed. Supervision can easily slip into an imbalance of examining only problem areas. Coming to supervision with a written checklist can help prioritize issues.
    B. When presenting artwork, bring the child's portfolio with you, organized chronologically. Introduce the work with a brief summary of the child's history and progress in expressive arts therapies. A quick

presentation and evaluation of the work should be followed by questions, concerns, goals, and possible directions for continuing treatment. It is recommended that expressive arts products and processes be presented during supervision at least once a month.

III. Maintaining Good Communication Between Supervisor(s), Co-leaders, Teachers, and Administration.

    A. Initiate brief meetings, written communication via staff mailbox systems or, if necessary, exchange home telephone numbers and set up specific phone-in times. Supervisees should take responsibility to maintain ongoing contact with professionals. Although this can be both time consuming and frustrating, it is an essential part of functioning within the system.

    B. In schools where expressive arts therapies is a new service being provided, classroom teachers may view it as a reward, privilege, or something extra that can be shifted around. The availability of art materials for personal expression can be misunderstood as play and indulgence. The complex task of relationship-building can be misunderstood as a special one-on-one time with an adult. A teacher might feel that a child should "earn" this time by attaching contingencies such as finishing classroom work before releasing a child to an expressive arts therapies appointment. Supervisees are advised to work with their supervisors to educate teachers regarding the professional nature of expressive arts therapies as a service that supports the child's educational goals.

    C. Early in the school year, create a mini expressive arts therapies in-service to educate teachers and support staff or meet individually with teachers in whose classes you will be working. Make available to teachers general treatment goals and a sample of group protocols. This will serve to generate interest, enthusiasm, and support for your work.

    D. Attend school meetings and functions such as individual education plans (IEP's), special education evaluation meetings, student support teams, staff meetings, open houses, parent teacher association meetings (PTA's) etc. Participating in these meetings provides supervisees with the opportunity to learn how systems within the school function and provides experience working within a team setting.

IV. Securing Space, Supplies and Storage

    A. Reserve rooms appropriate to the expressive arts modality for group and individual sessions.

    B. Discover ways to work within the classroom. Utilize screens to create private spaces for individual work. Make use of unusual spaces such as "cubby holes." Be prepared to compromise expectations for privacy from time to time.

C.   Volunteer to develop a budget proposal for the purchase of expressive arts supplies if your school does not have one allotted.

D.   Recruit donations from neighborhood shops. Bring a letter from the school stating your affiliation and the purpose of the expressive arts therapies program within the schools.

E.   Befriend the school's art, music, drama, physical education teachers, custodians, and secretarial staff who may have supplies and materials that they are willing to share with you. With approval of the appropriate school administrator, write to parents requesting various materials. Include everyone in the process of collecting supplies.

F.   Secure storage space for supplies or create a travel box enabling you to store supplies at home or in your car, if necessary.

V.   Maintaining Consistent Meeting Times with Children.

A.   Be prepared for a variety of interruptions–field trips, snow days, substitute teachers, absenteeism, suspension, sudden transfers to other school districts, injuries. Request that you be informed through the mailbox system with the expectation to arrange for a make-up session.

B.   Create flexibility in your schedule for make-up meetings. Arrange for a back-up meeting space, using the hallway or stairwell as a last resort to briefly meet with the child.

C.   If you are out sick, the same system applies. Inform your supervisor(s) and teachers whose children you are expected to see that day, by phone or through the mailbox system. Professional accountability for missed meetings is expected.

D.   School contracts run from September through June. Time off that does not follow the school calendar must be arranged with appropriate school personnel.

VI.   Direct Client Contact and Caseload Recommendations

A.   Supervisees are generally involved in direct service with children a minimum of 50 percent of the time. A caseload consisting of individual counseling, group counseling, psychoeducational activities and family work is recommended.

B.   Supervisees generally receive long-term, short-term, male and female referrals. Expect to encounter a variety of ages, presenting problems, and a diverse multicultural and socioeconomic population if you are in an urban school.

C. Keep your supervisor(s) informed when you are beginning and terminating treatment with children. Secure consent forms from parent or guardian when beginning treatment.

D. Children referred to expressive arts therapies are expected to keep their weekly appointments and stay for the full duration of the session. Keep a weekly log of scheduled appointments with children. This form should be shared weekly with your supervisor(s) so they are aware of your clinical caseload. Indicate missed appointments, abbreviated appointments, and rescheduled appointments. This will help to keep everyone informed about treatment taking place.

VII. Co-leading Expressive Arts Therapies, Counseling, and Psychoeducational Groups.

A. Initiate a variety of co-leadership experiences with other personnel. Look for opportunities to co-lead groups with expressive arts interns and staff from other disciplines such as: counseling psychology, social work, occupational therapy, psychology, special education and bilingual teachers, classroom teachers, and school counselors.

B. Schedule consistent weekly meetings to review groups and plan for the next group, by phone, if necessary.

C. It is recommended that supervisees receive co-leadership supervision by another clinician on a regular basis.

VIII. The Therapeutic Contract in Group Work

The therapeutic contract clarifies boundaries and expectations, protects group consistency, enhances the development of safety, and contributes to the building of trust. The therapeutic contract can be formally established in a brief interview prior to actually beginning a group or can take place during the first meeting. Contracts can be developed by the group leader or in a dialogue with children, a process that links treatment goals with expectations for group participation. The design of the therapeutic contract generally varies when applying to groups for young children and adolescent groups.

A. Group Description: name of group (reflecting the group's agenda); time; place; leadership; format; modality (e.g. art, music, movement, intermodal, etc.). Names of groups should be generic, simple, nonstigmatizing and nonthreatening, such as, examples: *Art Therapy for Grade Two Boys or Play with Clay.* Purposeful and 'catchy' names of groups are a critical factor in recruiting adolescent members. For example, *Proudly Protesting Peer Pressure* or the *"P" group.*

B. Confidentiality is an essential foundation for the building of a trusting therapeutic group experience. The limits of confidentiality (clear and imminent danger to the child or other people, and child abuse) should be explained clearly to children. The supervisee is advised to pay attention to the differing responses and reactions to the issue of confidentiality between children and adolescents.

Young children may confuse confidentiality with secrets and rely on the adult treators to communicate treatment issues to the team. It should also be explained that the child's permission must be secured in order to show artwork to parents or guardians.

Adolescents understand the concept of confidentiality, but still need things spelled out. Confidentiality in regard to information shared by another group member and its relationship to building trust in the group is particularly important for adolescents to understand.

C. Signing of Release Forms: the official format of a release can be frightening for a child or adolescent. Therefore, it is recommended to obtain releases before the group begins or after the members have bonded to allow the leader to address concerns students may have about signing the form.

Young children are minors and must have a parent or guardian sign the release form. Adolescents over age sixteen can sign their own forms.

D. Attendance and Termination: policy for missed groups; lateness; early departures.

Attendance accountability is typically not determined by the young child. However, policies for missed groups need to be instituted and may involve teacher cooperation in scheduling an individual make-up session, if appropriate.

Adolescents should be more accountable for consistency in school attendance. Policies for missed groups and appropriate contingencies need to be clarified.

E. Expectations for Participation: creating a continuum for the making of art and verbal communication.

If there is equal emphasis on both the making and talking about the art, then the art therapist needs to develop strategies to facilitate the child's ability to meet those expectations. For example, children might be asked to title their work or to use puppetry to act out a scene.

Resistances, inhibitions and fears all need to be explored when participation becomes problematic for adolescents.

F. Expectations for Ongoing Self-Assessment: client accountability in treatment; matching treatment goals with group participation.

For young children, the art therapist might gently insert a treatment goal into a discussion about behavior or in response to imagery, when appropriate.

For adolescents with the capacity to conceptualize treatment, treatment goals become important and useful reminders of why they are there. "Taking responsibility" for one's behavior is a developmentally relevant theme for the adolescent.

G. Storing the Art Work: where and for how long, and how and when the art work is to be returned to the client/artist.

Young children need to see concretely the portfolio that holds their work and where it will be stored, as well as to know that it will eventually be returned. On occasion, a child may need to take a piece or a duplicate of a piece home that very day.

Adolescents want to know who might see their work, and they want to know that it will be returned at an agreed upon date.

F. Group Difficulty: Reevaluating the appropriateness of group: disruptive behavior; inability to follow directions; inability to meet group expectations. These all lead to an evaluation of group "readiness." Group difficulty often becomes the reason for referral, not the reason for dismissal.

Socialization is inherently developmental. Issues of sharing, listening, and regression with materials might all be problematic for the young child.

Issues of power and control, artistic inhibition, or inappropriate sexual behavior might characterize adolescent issues in groups.

Guidelines for Supervisors

I. Pragmatic Issues Related to Supervising
   A. Help supervisees to problem-solve specific tasks early in the year, that maximize the supervisees presence in the school, setting the tone for a productive year (i.e. reserving an appropriate room for expressive arts therapies work with individuals and groups, stretching supply budgets, designing in-services, visiting classrooms, meeting specialists, forming good relationships with a variety of school personnel.)
   B. Assist supervisee with in-service planning.
   C. Assure caseload development.

II. Development of Work
   A. Educate supervisee about the stages of therapeutic work. This includes observation, initial relationship formation, deeper work, to termination. It also includes different types of work (behavioral improvement, emotional catharsis, etc.).
   B. Help supervisees to develop ideas for groups based on the needs of children referred into treatment.
   C. Educate the supervisee about the developmental stages of supervision.
   D. Contextualize the development as it parallels the development of the school year.
   E. Encourage supervisees to utilize the arts to invigorate the school and further interpersonal communication and group cooperation (i.e. developing behavior management strategies that are art-based; developing expressive arts and performance projects that foster group spirit and group cooperation, furthering communication between students and classes; utilizing artistic expression to celebrate diversity and multiculturalism, develop school spirit; create projects that link children to community).

III. Guiding the Learning Process
   A. Guides supervisees to better understand the unique role of expressive therapies in the schools.
   B. Identifies the learning needs of the supervisee and use teaching methods appropriate to supervisee's level of conceptual development, training, and experience.
   C. Helps supervisee with organization, planning, time management, record keeping, and reporting. This includes developing methods of monitoring work and appropriate documentation.
   D. Uses knowledge of gender, race, ethnicity, culture, and age to teach supervisee about how these differences may affect the use of expressive modalities and the development of the therapeutic relationship.

IV. Development of Skills in Expressive Arts Therapies
   A. Teaches supervisee about expressive arts therapies observation, assessment, analysis, and treatment planning.
   B. Helps develop ideas for groups based on the needs of students referred for treatment, linking expressive arts therapies goals to educational goals.
   C. Helps supervisee develop expressive arts therapies interventions through appropriate examples. These include: role play, suggestions, modeling, using expressive arts therapies in supervision, reviewing tapes.

D. Teach the supervisee to use expressive arts therapies to deepen his/her understanding of the child's process and bring awareness to his/her own process as an expressive arts therapist.

V. Topics for Discussion in Supervision

Although the content of supervision is developed in response to the work, sometimes supervision serves to direct the work. Many topics are routinely discussed and typically follow a calendar progression. Examples of such topics are as follows:

A. **Hellos and good-byes:** developing exercises that support transitions into and out of treatment for the different age groups. Concretization of entering and exiting treatment happens by putting together portfolios and arranging to store the artwork, reviewing and returning the artwork.

B. **Thematic development:** what to explore, with what age groups. The supervisor can assist the supervisee to develop a notebook of exercises to have on hand, considering: week-to-week continuity, resistance, underlying issues, long-term and short-term goals and long-term and short-term projects.

C. **Understanding the image:** noting repetitions, distortions, developmental indicators, and pictorial content. Discover a variety of methods to: elicit associations, help a child develop a story line, identify a wish or fear, or move on to the next image.

D. **Structuring the session:** ritualizing these beginnings and endings, with special attention to developing and attending to "closure" at the end of a session. Sometimes, snacks are offered to children at the close of a session. This can replenish the child's energy, creates a quiet time for talking, reinforce the nurturing aspects of therapy, and supplement a missed breakfast. Typically, there is no budget to cover the cost. Having a snack can also open up a whole new arena of boundary issues and struggles. It is also important to determine the degree of involvement in set up and clean up of having snacks from a therapeutic point of view.

E. **Client/therapist relationship:** establishing contracts, developing a therapeutic alliance, setting goals, boundaries and limits.

F. **The process/product continuum:** determining when expressive arts therapies should be a self-directed exploration of the expressive arts products or a more guided and focused exploration of an idea presented by the expressive arts therapist.

G. **Transference and countertransference issues:** directed toward the child/therapist relationship, and toward the expressive arts products and processes.

H. **Suspected Child Abuse:** discussing issues related to instances of abuse and neglect which can be disclosed by children verbally or appear in the imagery of their work. The process of reporting suspected abuse needs to be discussed early on in the supervisory relationship. Suspected abuse needs to be reported promptly by the appropriate school personnel. In some cases, this is the therapist or the school principal. As suspected child abuse is a very serious and emotionally charged issue, supervisors can help supervisees by carefully guiding them through the steps of reporting.

Discussing Difficult Topics in Supervision

A supervisor and supervisee can expect to encounter periodic tension and resistance in discussing difficult or emotionally charged topics during the course of a supervisory relationship. Addressing the development of professional goals as an ongoing process within the context of a trusting supervisory relationship can help to diffuse feelings of judgment and blame between supervisor and supervisee when they arise. The ability to engage in a reciprocal dialogue which encourages the giving and receiving of feedback is a necessary professional goal between supervisor and supervisee.

Below is a list of topics describing important aspects of professional development to be discussed in supervision. Using this list as a point of departure, a supervisor can encourage a supervisee to make his or her own list. This process encourages a collaborative approach to issues which might otherwise feel isolating and judgmental to the supervisee.

- Dependability and consistency
- Motivation
- Initiative
- Resourcefulness and problem-solving capacity
- Self-confidence, management of anxiety
- Flexibility
- Organizational ability
- Communication skill, assertiveness
- Leadership ability
- Appropriateness of dress and interaction
- Confidentiality
- Observational skills
- Creativity
- Expressive arts therapist's ability to inspire exploration and expression
- Relationships with students
- Empathic capacity
- Ability to set boundaries

- Relationships with professionals and peers
- Ability to accept feedback
- Ability to give feedback

Figure 3: L. K. R., age 8.

Chapter 3

CASE MANAGEMENT GUIDELINES

Case Management and Structural Guidelines

The management of client data is an important professional responsibility. The amount of data required, as well as the manner in which data are to be recorded in client files, varies from institution, agency, or school. Schools can be particularly challenging regarding their policies, or lack there of, to include and organize clinical information in school files about a child's treatment. Supervisors and supervisees alike are encouraged to have a file for each child they see in treatment. When carefully developed and organized, this file can serve as a quick reference to assist in the summarization and evaluation of treatment. Developing documentation and case management forms, as well as, good report writing skills are particularly important when they become a part of a child's school record.

Description of Case Management Forms

Weekly Log

The weekly log provides the on-site and off-site supervisors with a quick overview of the supervisees weekly schedule. It is designed to track (1) meeting times as well as missed appointments with children, supervisors, and teachers; (2) time spent documenting treatment; preparation time for clinical work; and (3) time spent attending in-service seminars. The log informs supervisors of scheduling issues, the supervisee's weekly caseload, overall program delivery and documentation, and patterns of communication and collaboration with teachers and co-leaders.

Referral Form

The referral form which is generally filled out by teachers provides supervisees with background information about the children referred for treatment. Without the use of this form, information is often delivered to the supervisees in anecdotal fragments. The referral form specifies clinical information upon which to build a treatment plan, including: presenting problems; reason for referral to expressive arts therapies; an overview of the child's personal and family history; school performance; peer relationships; and recommended treatment goals. The form also aids supervisees in a large system, riddled with change and crisis, by identifying a contact person for a quick exchange of pertinent information from week to week.

Process Note

The process note helps supervisees to conceptualize the treatment. It directs them to practice organized and thoughtful reporting and to officially document sessions. The note contains behavioral observations such as attendance, attitude, level of involvement, task skills, and transitions to and from group or individual sessions. The note also provides a forum to discuss the psychodynamic content of each session, the use of imagery; group membership; relationships with peers and group leader; and transference and countertransference issues.

Group Protocol

The group protocol provides a standardized format to describe a range of expressive arts therapies services. The format states group title (reflecting the group's agenda); group description; goals; and referral criteria. It forms the basis for the group contract. The group protocol quickly informs teachers about the content of the group, the appropriateness of members, and the procedure for referral.

Mini-Case Presentation Format

The mini-case presentation format combines the referral form with the process note, creating an organized context from which to view the art. The outline format assists the supervisee in organizing an orderly presentation of the expressive arts products. All of the relevant information becomes available for discussion, as supervisee and supervisor search for the layers of meaning held by the image and execution of the work.

Release Form

The release form is a standard form in most practices, however, both the designing of a release form and the signing of the form can stir up many reactions in school settings. The release form is a legal document written to protect the client/artist, the expressive arts products, and the practicing expressive arts therapist. In order for this document to be effective, it must be written clearly, covering all contingencies. It is important to note that the clinical and legalistic language of the release form may need clarifying for children, parents and guardians. Some families may be unwilling to sign such a form until they have developed a trusting relationship with the expressive arts therapist or intern. From the point of view of the expressive arts therapist or intern, the release form, holding specific reference to the expressive arts products, must be signed before the treatment begins.

Termination Reports

The termination report provides a concise summary of clinical work done over a specific period of time. Within the school system, these documents can supply information needed to offer continuous care for those students in need.

For a supervisee, the report furnishes a record of the clinical work accomplished. The process of writing the report is a necessary and invaluable piece of training. It offers the supervisee a different way to review the expressive arts therapy treatment that s/he has guided during the year. As such, the termination report becomes an important part of the supervisee's termination process.

Figure 4: K. L., age 7 1/2.

Chapter 4

COLLABORATION AND COMMUNICATION
GUIDELINES

Establishing Consistent School-Wide and System-Wide Policies

The establishment of consistent school-wide or system-wide policies varies from school system to school system. Many schools are aware of a need for an improved system of communication particularly as intraprofessional collaboration increases. Other schools are in need of communication guidelines, however, they may be lacking in the necessary commitment and leadership to put such guidelines in place. For supervisees learning the school's guidelines (or lack thereof) around key areas is essential in their understanding of how the system works (or doesn't). The guidelines described below are intended to be examples of how a particular school system might structure certain policies and guidelines.

Guidelines for Meetings with Families of Children Receiving Expressive Arts Therapies Services

A. **The recommended first contact** with families should be in the form of a letter sent home at the start of the school year, informing parents of the expressive arts therapies services available to children.

B. **The second contact** is often a phone call to the families of children referred into treatment. The supervisee explains the reasons for referral of the child, and goals of treatment to the parent or guardian requesting permission for their child to be included in the expressive arts therapies services. This should be followed up at a later date with an official release form.

C. **"Check-in" telephone calls** with families, perhaps occurring monthly or at mid-year are recommended. Additional calls might be needed for clarification of issues or situations that arise during the year. For example, changing the treatment with the child from individual to dyad or group; or in response to a school-based, family-based, or community-based crisis; deteriorating school performance; or a change in behavior. It is also important for parents to be notified of positive changes in their child's behavior and performance.

D. **Face-to-face meetings** are set-up from time to time to deepen alliances with the family or to clarify information or issues that cannot be handled effectively over the phone. Meetings with families can be complex in nature, it is therefore recommended that another professional participate in meetings, if necessary. A triad meeting format varies and typically includes: supervisees, parents, counselor or teacher, principal or specialist.

E. **Home visits** in most public schools are rare occurrences. They are arranged by and take place with the school counselor and family. Home visits would be indicated if a child's school performance is deteriorating in conjunction with symptomatic behavior indicating increased levels of stress or trauma. Home visits may also be indicated with families who appear resistant to attend meetings at the school. The family may present as uninvolved, unavailable, without phone, unresponsive to letters sent home. Until an in-person meeting is set up, it is difficult to know the reason a family may be reluctant to attend meetings at school.

F. **Information that relates to the goals of treatment** should be shared with parents in an effort to include them in the larger "educational" process as allies of their child's welfare. However, boundary issues and issues of confidentiality must be respected as supervisees go about building and maintaining a trusting relationship with the children being seen. For example, children need to give the supervisee permission before their expressive arts products can be shown to parents.

Guidelines for Handling Discipline

A series of interventions for handling routine discipline problems should be discussed and developed in supervision. Serious problems such as hitting, throwing things, or threatening behavior are frequently handled in the following manner.

A. Children that exhibit disruptive behavior which interferes with the group's ability to maintain a task focus should be given warnings or check's before being sent to the principal's office or other designated office in the school. Disruptive children should never be sent directly back to the classroom. An additional consequence of disruptive behavior might be to have the child lose recess privileges. However, the goal would be to try to keep the child in the treatment experience since the acting-out behavior indicates that the child needs the services being provided.

B. The supervisee should check back with the child in the principal's office after the group and briefly meet with the teacher to explain the situation.

Guidelines for Identifying and Reporting Suspected Abuse

A. Supervisees are mandated to report suspected abuse. Schools should have clearly stated reporting procedures. In most cases, suspected abuse or neglect is reported by supervisees to their supervisor and then to the school principal. It is preferable to have the principal file the actual report since s/he is generally not actively involved in the treatment of the child or family as is the supervisee or supervisor. The filing takes place after first informing the parents.

B. It is also recommended that supervisees take an investigatory step by calling the Department of Social Service (or appropriate state agency) to describe the situation in order to determine whether it would indeed qualify as suspected abuse. This can be done without identifying the names of any of the individuals involved.

Guidelines For Exhibiting Expressive Arts Products

Expressive arts therapists are increasingly engaged in coordinating expressive arts exhibitions. Widening exposure to the field of expressive arts therapies, securing outside funding, and celebrating artistic expression often motivate these experiences.

Exhibitions are complex events to organize. They require numbers of decisions and arrangements to be made months in advance of the actual exhibition date. The following set of guidelines outlines specific considerations and arrangements that need to be made. Planning and pacing the various tasks associated with staging an exhibition will benefit all participants and can be adapted to group performances Below is a listing of tasks and considerations that are organized chronically. However, many of these tasks should be developed simultaneously.

A. **Create an exhibition committee** to determine the scope and coordinate the exhibition event. Membership on the committee should include professionals within the school in an effort to diversify, as well as define, exhibition goals. Ideally, the committee should be co-chaired by an expressive arts therapy intern and an expressive arts therapy supervisor, school-based counselor, school or expressive arts therapy program administrator, or teacher.

B. **Determine the scope and purpose of the exhibition.** Expressive arts therapy interns often define their role within the schools from a fairly narrow perspective. The development of the intern's vision of expressive arts therapy during the early months of a placement influences how s/he steps out and beyond the "closed door metaphor of treatment" to engage larger groups of children in expressive work. This includes work that fosters multicultural goals, interdisciplinary possibilities, and moral development. Creating an exhibition event can rally school spirit, create a positive meeting ground between families and schools, and bring the multiple benefits of expressive arts therapy work into focus for all to witness. Creating a title and theme that reflects the goals of the program is a great and exciting challenge for the committee.

C. **Determine the population to be represented by the exhibition,** including the following:

- All or some of the children referred for treatment (with appropriate releases in place);
- Interested classrooms or groups of students within the school to participate as a whole unit, following the inclusion model, without identifying children specifically referred to expressive arts therapy treatment;
- After-school programs; or
- Children invited to submit selected work of their own initiative

D. **Determine criteria for exhibiting expressive arts products and processes:** aesthetic merit, noteworthy creative or expressive work, work that holds psychological significance, work that is representative of group effort, or thematic consistency. It can challenge the most seasoned expressive arts therapist to combine the implied therapeutic contract of empathic, positive regard for all images with the establishment of value-laden criteria for aesthetic or creative judgment.

E. **Create a timetable of tasks to be accomplished.** Delegate responsibility to various committee members. Keep in mind that committee members are typically volunteers who take on this "extra" piece of work. Often their initial enthusiasm for such a grand event fades quickly into feeling overwhelmed by the concerns of the clinical work. Maintain ongoing communication through written up-dates and periodic meetings. Most importantly, maintain the timetable set up by the committee.

F. **Secure exhibition space.** A local setting away from the school elevates the formality of the exhibition and creates an air of celebration and festivity. City halls, museums, malls, corporations, are potentially appropriate settings. Sites with active commercial traffic will increase program exposure. Anticipate the amount of work to be displayed and the size of space needed. If a performance piece is to be included, space must accommodate such an event. A reasonable time frame to exhibit work is from two weeks to a month. Secure all dates in writing.

G. **Determine avenues for publicity and appropriate press coverage.** Explore a variety of sources to advertise the event: school newspapers, local newspapers, college bulletins, radio stations announcing cultural events of the week, local cable TV channels. Press coverage may be in the form of advertisement prior to the event, attendance at the opening, or a review of the event. Other kinds of coverage can include in-depth newspaper articles that feature the overall program, its purpose and evolution within the school, making special note of the upcoming exhibition.

H. **Confidentially must be carefully considered and discussed when formulating an exhibition of client art.** The issue of confidentiality can polarize committee members, school administrators, parents, and affiliating college faculty. Getting publicity for such a large event may lead to increased program recognition, new potential funding sources for expanding services, and a heightened investment in the work by all participating professionals. However, publicity can also invade the privacy of the client/artist, compromise confidentiality, risk exploitation, and alienate families from the professionals. Alternatively, public recognition can elevate low self-esteem, and nurture group collaboration and spirit.

I. **Create release forms** that specify exhibiting art work and/or the release of nonidentifying information to be included as part of the publicity or press coverage for the event. Children are minors and cannot comprehend all of the issues at stake. A letter to parents and guardians explaining the purpose of the exhibit, along with a phone number to answer questions, should accompany the release forms.

J. **Seek special funding or donations** of materials and refreshments for the exhibition event; this is sometimes the first consideration on a committee's agenda. Banks, corporations, and local grocery stores often offer small grants to local projects that benefit the immediate community, furthering educational, artistic, or multicultural goals. Local stores particularly appreciate acknowledgment at the event and view it as an opportunity to advertise community involvement. Create an exhibition budget that includes: materials needed to hang the work (mats, tape, hangers); expenses associated with printing invitations and fliers; postage for mailings; food and beverages for the opening; film to document the event; blank video cassettes to document performance pieces; and the cost of transportation for families.

K. **Designing an attractive flier** is a critical detail in developing an exhibition event. A flier is a valuable advertisement for the larger purpose of the program. Fliers can contain information about who is eligible for services and how to apply for and receive services. Fliers can acknowledge efforts by particular individuals and donations by corporations or neighborhood stores.

L. **Define opportunities for parental participation.** Generating enthusiasm for the event is key to parental involvement. Parents can be encouraged to assist in seeking local donations (food, hanging materials, art materials), helping with the mailings, baking cookies and cakes for the opening, and acting as welcoming figures at the opening for families who may be hesitant to attend such an event.

M. **Consider the specific secretarial tasks connected with the event.** These include: design and printing of fliers and invitations; tags with names of artists and titles of work represented in the exhibit; and artists' statements or descriptions of the work. It is also important to mount descriptions of the program and write various letters to secure the exhibition space and donations of materials. Other letters are written to parents and school officials explaining the purpose of the exhibit, and thank you notes are sent to all participants, committee members, volunteers, and interns associated with the event. Finally, various mailings are sent at the different stages of exhibition planning.

N. **Prepare for an "art opening".** Determining the time of year, time of day, and day of the week, is all very important in planning for a well-attended event. Assume that there is no ideal time that will work equally well for children, families, educators, interns, supervisors, administrators, city officials, and college faculty at the affiliating college. In selecting a season, spring typically represents a time of great productivity for interns and children. However, end of semester pressures build at the time that is most suitable for planning an exhibition. In anticipating the demanding nature of planning an exhibition, it is important to plan to complete most of the work in advance. Preparing a participatory art experience for the opening can be fun. A simple task, ritualizing the entry or departure from the event, can work to further enliven the experience.

O. **Invitations** identify the place, time of day, day of the week, the artists, and refreshments offered. When sending invitations to the families of children involved in the program, special arrangement for transportation to the exhibition should be considered. Organizing carpools or creating a small van shuttle can greatly increase the attendance. Invitations should be mailed to: all families of children represented in the exhibition; all families of children referred into treatment; teachers, interns, school administrators, city officials, faculty at the affiliating college; and all supervisors participating in the program.

P. **Visit the exhibition space prior to actually hanging the work.** Find out what custodial assistance is available, what system is in place for hanging work (panels, specific wall space, etc.), whether nails are allowed or what types of hanging materials are recommended, and whether pedestals or display cases are available. Plan a date well in advance of the hanging for the work to be delivered, matted or framed appropriately, and stored. Plan generously for many hours to be spent pulling the work together and hanging the art work at the exhibition site.

Q. **Complete the final task,** which involves taking work down, returning individual pieces to children, and determining permanent installation sites for the group work. It is by far the simplest task, but still one important to anticipate and plan. Walls of the exhibition site may also need touch up after the art is removed. Transportation and storage may also be needed.

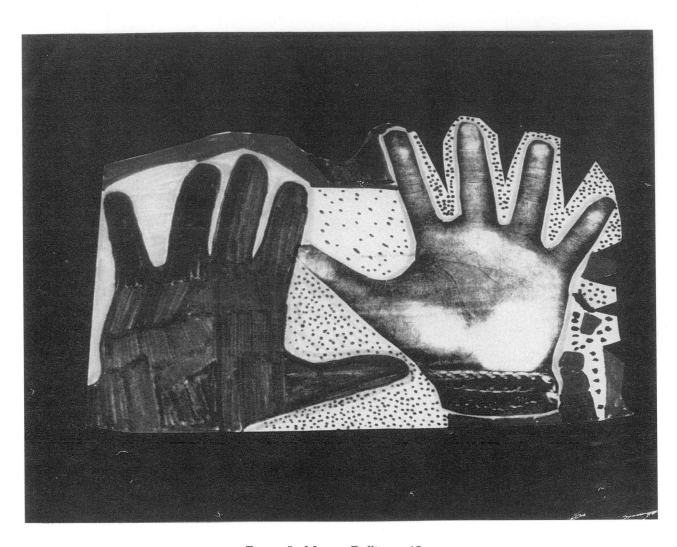

Figure 5: Marcus Dalli, age 15.

Chapter 5

OBSERVATION AND EVALUATION:
PROCESS AND PROCEDURES

Observations

Observations and evaluations by supervisors can be complex aspects in the training of interns and supervisees that need to be understood fully by all parties. An observation can occur spontaneously, but typically is arranged in advance by the intern/supervisee. An observation provides the supervisor with a firsthand encounter of a single session with a child or group, conducted by the supervisee.

Observation by the supervisor of the intern/supervisee working directly with children informs the supervisor of how the work is going, i.e., how the supervisee interacts with children and responds to a range of behaviors. Through the supervisor's observation of the multiple interactions and nuances of nonverbal communication that take place between child and therapist, interns/supervisees can feel the most understood in their striving to become competent expressive arts therapists. Observations also provide supervisees with a rich opportunity to receive important feedback from their supervisor.

Observation Guidelines

Facilitating a nonintrusive observational experience can be challenging. The very act of 'observing' changes the dynamics between child and intern/supervisee. The following guidelines can assist both intern/supervisee and supervisor in setting the stage for an observation.

A. Although the presence of a supervisor in the room can initially stir self-consciousness in both intern/supervisee and child, soon both become immersed in the work and become a bit more relaxed. Supervisors take this phenomenon into account when observing interns/supervisees working with children and often expect children to present a range of behaviors: pseudo-cooperative, attention-seeking, defiant, charming, disruptive, uneasy. The supervisor is most interested in getting a "flavor" for the child, in determining whether the intern/supervisee has a real handle on whom she or he is working with, and in noting how the intern/supervisee responds to whatever behavior emerges.

B. Supervisors are not expected to co-lead a session with the intern/supervisee, but rather to be a kind of "invisible," pleasant presence in the room. Sometimes an intern/supervisee may look to his or her supervisor for assistance or guidance during a particularly difficult session. Two contradictory facts are important for both supervisor and intern/supervisee to keep in mind: (1) that children's safety is of paramount concern, and (2) that the supervisor remain in his or her role as an observer.

C. The intern/supervisee should inform their child or group, a week in advance, that his/her supervisor will be observing the meeting time. Interns can explain to children that s/he is also in school and that his/her supervisor is a kind of 'teacher'. The interns/supervisees should introduce the child or group to the supervisor and provide an unobtrusive seat for the supervisor. The supervisor should then refrain from interacting with the child or group. At the close of the session, the intern/supervisee can model a simple goodbye to his/her supervisor, as s/he transitions the child or group back to the classroom.

D. The supervisor should expect to observe a session for the full meeting time. Transitions to and from sessions are important segues which often require therapeutic skills and behavior management and can be useful as part of the observation.

E. The intern/supervisee and supervisor should discuss in advance which child or group it would be the most helpful to observe. This decision is based upon what would be most instrumental to the intern's/supervisee's development as a clinician. Sometimes it is important for a supervisor to see work that is going smoothly, empowering the intern/supervisee with positive feedback. It can also be argued that, because observations typically occur only a few times a year, they should be used primarily to problem-solve difficulties between the child and therapist. The supervisor should ask the intern/supervisee about what s/he is most concerned, specifically what s/he would like to be the focus of the supervisor, and the kind of feedback that would be most helpful. The supervisor may want to revisit a group at a later date for a better understanding of changes that have or have not taken place.

F. Observations made over the course of the year should take into consideration the range of treatment relationships that exist at the site. The supervisor should schedule a representative range: individual, dyads, groups, difficult relationships, productive relationships, caring relationships.

G. Scheduling difficulties often determine who gets seen during an observation. Typically the supervisor puts aside the one hour for supervision when the intern/supervisee is scheduled to meet with the supervisor, not with a child or a group. Individual children are easier to reschedule than a group.

It is necessary for the supervisor to be as flexible as possible, so as to accommodate a group meeting time. Sometimes this cannot be done. Because of the scheduling dilemma, the supervisor and intern/supervisee can expect to encounter some tension over arranging for an observation.

Observations and Feedback

It is not uncommon that intern/supervisee will experience feelings of ambivalence about being observed. On the one hand, s/he appreciates receiving specific, experienced feedback. On the other hand, s/he may fear that they will be judged and criticized.

Separating observations from evaluations is essential to creating a safe climate and a sense of trust between intern/supervisee and supervisor. Although observations can occur without being linked to evaluations, the two often come together. The delivery of feedback after an observation sets the tone for the interaction. The following considerations can be taken into account:

A. Following an observation, the intern/supervisee and supervisor should meet for half an hour to review the session, while it is fresh in the minds of both of them. Ideally, feedback is designed to motivate an intern/supervisee to a new level of awareness and professionalism about the work, rather than to discourage the intern/supervisee from the work. If possible, feedback should be balanced by positives and addressing the challenges..

B. It is important for both the supervisor and the intern/supervisee to keep in mind that, at times, the supervisor can appear to "forget" that the intern/supervisee is just learning and may be swept away by the emotional price of a mistake. The intern's/supervisee's professional development can be overshadowed by the mistake that, under the scrutiny of observation, seems to get magnified out of proportion to the moment.

Interns often lack role modeling around mistakes. Case studies in books typically portray the therapist as competent, if not omnipotent or flawless. The college instructor often describes difficult cases retrospectively from the perspective of competent, clinical judgment. Learning from our mistakes necessitates that we recognize them and are compassionate about making mistakes. Supervisors must model compassion as they attempt to understand the psychodynamic issues that contribute to the intern's/supervisee's judgment.

C. The supervisor may deliver feedback in a variety of formats:

- React to what takes place in the session;
- Assist the intern/supervisee to reflect more fully on what the client is doing or feeling;
- Illustrate dynamics observed with vignettes from his/her own clini-

cal practice;
- Suggest readings that will better inform the intern/supervisee about an aspect of the work observed;
- Problem-solve new directions or interventions that will aid the work with the child.

D. It is also appropriate for the supervisor to receive feedback from the intern/supervisee from time to time. This feedback can be difficult to facilitate because of the difference in power between intern/supervisee and supervisor. It is important that the intern/supervisee feel a sense of permission to give feedback. It is also important that the supervisor communicate that the feedback by the intern/supervisee will contribute to their mutual well-being and development.

Evaluations

Evaluations can be formal or informal. They can occur every few months or be an ongoing aspect of supervision. They can be one-sided, coming from the supervisor, or they can be elicited from the intern/supervisee as well, as a thoughtful reflection of his/her own performance. A calendar progression exists in regard to an intern's/supervisee's perception of performance and a supervisor's expectation of performance.

Difficult Evaluations

The supervisor depends on the intern's/supervisee's ability to report experience accurately. However, without observing an his/her performance with children, the supervisor never really gets a full flavor of what takes place.

Most often, what is observed resembles what has been reported. Sometimes, however, that is not the case. It is of particular concern when the supervisor encounters a very worrisome situation in which the intern/supervisee is conducting the work in an unsafe or unethical manner. The following are examples of troubling situations:

1. The intern/supervisee is unable to control or direct the experience.
2. The intern/supervisee engages in inappropriate physical contact.
3. There is a breakdown of boundaries on the part of the intern/supervisee, who may engage in a series of inappropriate personal disclosures.
4. The intern/supervisee may show a lack of empathic regard for the child.
5. The intern/supervisee may manifest overt racism.

6. The intern/supervisee may engage in 'Splitting' with the team.
7. The intern/supervisee may encourages primitive regression with materials or excessive wastefulness.
8. The intern/supervisee may be unable to begin or end a session on time or within a reasonable time frame.
9. Objects such as scissors or furniture are thrown around the room; children are unresponsive to limits set by the intern/supervisee.
10. Children are openly stealing materials.
11. A sense of distrust permeates the session.

Structures and consequences must be in place to respond effectively and immediately. These include:

1. Reducing the caseload;
2. Changing the meeting format with the more difficult children, reducing the size of the groups, or reducing the time of the meetings;
3. Arranging for an experienced co-leader to role model therapeutic interventions;
4. Making specific behavioral recommendations and setting up a follow-up observation to evaluate implementation;
5. Possibly terminating the intern's contract in the case of serious ethical violations.

Conditions Warranting Termination of an Intern's Contract

The termination of an intern's contract is a rare occurrence. Supervisors and sites train interns with the understanding that interns are in the role of a "learner" and that good clinical judgment is an evolving process. On rare occasions, however, an intern may display behaviors that are considered to be unethical, irresponsible, or reckless, placing a child or intern in jeopardy. Some examples may include:

1. Repeatedly miss appointments;
2. Engage in inappropriate physical contact;
3. Poor personal and professional boundaries;
4. Behave in a manner that is unresponsive and damaging to children's needs.

The termination of an intern's contract typically occurs when previous attempts to resolve these issues have failed.

Figure 6: K. L., age 7 1/2.

Chapter 6

PROFESSIONAL DEVELOPMENT

Credentialing and Licensing

The credentialing of expressive arts therapists has been a major trend in the last few decades. Credentialing activities include certification, licensure, and accreditation of educational programs. While not universally accepted as necessary or even desirable, credentialing and licensure helps to ensure basic standards with regard to qualifications, educational competence, and training experience. In the long run, it is likely that credentialing and licensure will do much to enhance the credibility and visibility of expressive arts therapists. Credentialing and licensure provides greater exposure and rights for expressive arts therapists in such areas as employment, third-party reimbursement from insurance companies and some government agencies. Credentialing and licensure can also help to support the professional identity of expressive arts therapists. As credentialing and licensure varies from state to state, it is recommended that expressive arts therapists become active in advancing their profession on state and national levels by becoming advocates and activists to ensure that expressive arts therapists have greater access to practice their profession.

Continued Professional Development as a Clinician

In general, expressive arts therapists are very committed to developing clinical competencies. Since expressive arts therapists incorporate a number of different theoretical frameworks into their work, there is a tremendous variety of resources to explore.

Continuing Education

Expressive arts therapists attend conferences and workshops in a variety of disciplines in an effort to increase clinical skills. In addition, licensing eligibility and requirements require that expressive arts therapists, like other professionals, continue to study and develop new ideas within their fields, accumulating a particular number of CE's (continuing education credits) for licensure renewal. Finding appropriate workshops or conferences to attend is a fairly easy process.

1. By joining and receiving newsletters from a number of different professional associations, expressive arts therapists will find themselves on a number of mailing lists and will automatically receive many unsolicited workshop announcements.

2. Colleges and universities with large psychology or expressive arts therapy departments often sponsor conferences or institutes.

3. Each expressive arts therapy discipline—art, music, dance, psychodrama—schedules national conferences each year in different locations across the country.

4. Other organizations, such as: the psychoanalytic societies, psychotherapy institutes, and group therapy associations, all schedule annual national conferences held at rotating locations.

Membership in Professional Associations

"Networking" has become an essential aspect of professional survival. Membership in professional associations benefit members in the following ways:

1. It brings expressive arts therapists into contact with each other, creating a sense of support, reducing a sense of isolation.

2. It creates a forum to discuss shared concerns.

3. It creates a forum to develop a number of issues:

- lobbying for better political representation;
- creating a core group of volunteers to organize a regional conference or workshop;
- developing ideas for a panel at a national conference.

4. It brings professionals into contact with each other who can produce new alliances, including peer supervision groups or private practice affiliations.

5. Many professional associations represent members at different phases of their careers. Professional associations can offer new graduates mentoring opportunities as they come into contact with senior clinicians.

6. It is also recommended that expressive arts therapists become members in national counseling associations whose practices and codes of ethics are generally followed in school-based counseling. The two national counseling associations are the American Counseling Association and the American Mental Health Counselors Association.

Peer Supervision Groups

Peer supervision groups have become a valuable resource for a clinician's continued development. Peer supervision groups can be social gatherings that provide clinicians with an opportunity to present case work and receive competent feedback from colleagues.

1. Peer supervision reduces the isolation of expressive arts therapists, either in private practice or working as a sole department within a hospital system.

2. Peer supervision is an economical way to promote reflection and continued development as a professional. It can provide feedback, suggestions, and moral support. When members feel safe with one another, peer supervision can provide an opportunity to explore countertransference issues and to clarify other clinical blinds spots.

3. Peer supervision can also become a source of referrals from colleagues.

Subscriptions to Professional Journals

Many expressive arts therapists are skillful at writing about their work. There is a proliferation of journals, newsletters and bulletins that keep clinicians informed about changes in credentialing, research and assessment, theoretical ideas under debate, and program development. A comprehensive listing of the different expressive arts therapy journals includes the following:

> *Art Therapy: Journal of the American Art Therapy Association*
> *Arts in Psychotherapy*
> *The American Journal of Art Therapy*
> *American Journal of Dance Therapy*
> *Journal of Music Therapy*
> *Music Therapy*
> *International Journal of Arts Medicine*
> *Psychodrama Therapy*
> *Journal of Poetry Therapy*

Continued Professional Development Within One's Modality

It is very important that expressive arts therapists give equal time to developing their artistic competencies in the same way they devote time to developing their clinical skills. Developing skills in one's modality requires substantial effort and commitment. Akin to how we develop expressive arts therapy skills as clinicians (i.e., taking courses, attending conferences, joining professional organizations, and forming peer supervision groups), the art world also presents as multifaceted and requires some navigational expertise. Exploring the different aspects of professional development as an artist can occur simultaneously or be charted as a developmental progression, with each step validating preceding steps.

The fields of art, music, dance, and theatre have many opportunities for expressive arts therapists to explore their skills. Outlined below are possible directions for expressive arts therapists to take in an effort to expand their competencies and professional identities as artists. Although this listing primarily identifies options for visual artists, parallel opportunities exist within the other modalities.

1. **Organizational Support:** Perhaps because visual artists are more likely to work in isolation, compared to musicians, dancers, and theatre performers, and because visual artists are the least protected by copyright laws, a variety of support systems have recently emerged between artists. Community art associations, cooperative galleries, artist's unions, political organizations (Women's Caucus for the Arts, Artists for Political and Social Justice), serve to network artists to each other. Many arts organizations are poorly funded. If membership dues are collected at all, they are nominal so as not to exclude artists with small incomes. Therefore, many arts organizations are not listed in phone books, and are difficult to track down, except by word of mouth. Sometimes arts colleges post information about arts organizations, or local art stores can be a source for this kind of information. Some organizations are beginning to appear as web sites on the Internet.

2. **Community Support:** Some towns are willing to sponsor artists through seasonal events: outdoor exhibits; city street arts events; craft fairs; "arts in the park" programs. Some artists prefer to begin their involvement as volunteers, helping to facilitate the event. City Hall personnel in most towns and cities are able to provide names of people to contact.

3. **Continuing Education:** Learning new techniques, exploring new media, developing new skills, further refining old skills, changing directions, and digging more deeply are all part of continued development as artists. This process can occur in many forms: professional workshops, college summer institutes, classes held at centers for adult education, community colleges, universities, community art centers, arts studios in the form of "open life drawing studios" where artists share the cost of the model, private lessons; tutorials.

4. **Support Groups:** Artists are forming critique groups (just like peer supervision groups) to gain feedback about their work, have potlucks, share slides, or book groups to decrease a sense of isolation.

5. **Exhibitions of Work for Juried or Nonjuried Shows:** Every community has both traditional gallery space and alternative gallery space. Some

alternative spaces include: libraries, banks; bookstores, frame shops, art stores, churches or synagogues; restaurants, cafes, movie theatres, hair salons. Many corporations and colleges use lobby space for art or have actual gallery space to offer to artists seeking to display their work. Many cooperative galleries, community arts programs or sometimes regional museums, sponsor annual competitions to represent local artists. The alternative spaces are usually not insured, however, they sometimes help artists to defray the cost of exhibiting work by providing bulk mailings or sending out press releases to various newspapers.

6. **Curatorial Opportunities:** Many alternative exhibition spaces are receptive to curatorial proposals put forth by artists or nonartists. With the arrival of "outsider art," along with explicitly psychological and/or political art, audiences encounter a range of images and installations in their viewing of art, and they are excited about these new art forms.

7. **Regional Arts Journals or Newspapers:** As the art world has decentralized away from major metropolitan areas, becoming more regional, small journals or newspapers for artists have emerged to review shows, interview artists, and list local competitions. These same journals also advertise photographers who, for a fee, will take professional slides of art work. Creating one's own library of slides to document the progression of work is a fundamental bridge between the private world of art-making and the public world of exhibiting your work.

Although the resources listed above are primarily related to the visual art world, many of these ideas can be transferred to other modalities. For example, art can be displayed in cafes, and music can be played in cafes. Also, children's programs are rapidly expanding with new opportunities for performing artists. The important message for expressive arts therapists is not to get discouraged. There is support for artists, and that support reinforces the importance of making art or performing art within one's modality.

Figure 7: L. K. R., age 8.

Chapter 7

GUIDELINES FOR INTRODUCING AND PROMOTING EXPRESSIVE ARTS THERAPIES IN SCHOOL SETTINGS

Recommendations for Contacting Schools To Explore Consulting, Employment or Training Opportunities in Expressive Arts Therapies

Linking up with a Graduate School of Art, Dance, Music, or Expressive Arts Therapies if One is Located in Your Area

If you are an expressive arts therapist and you live near a graduate school which offers expressive arts therapies training contact them and inquire if they place students in public schools. If they do, ask about the supervision model in place and explore if there is a place for you as a supervisor within this model. If they don't, see if they are interested in developing a collaboration with public schools and offer some of your ideas and suggestions about the establishment of such a collaboration. See if they would be interested in working with you to approach the school system.

Becoming Employed by Public School Systems

Depending on what state you reside in, there are different qualifications necessary to be employed by a school but it is generally either department of education certification as a school counselor or psychologist or state licensure as a counselor, social worker, or psychologist. If you are an expressive arts therapist trainee or professional interested in working in a school (and your particular state does not include expressive arts therapies certification within it's school department employment hiring requirements) research what additional qualifications might be necessary to enable you to be hired by a public school.

Getting into a School System When You Don't Have the Required Credentials

Like all societal institutions today schools are going through tremendous change, restructuring, and transformation. Now is a good time to approach schools with an innovative plan to provide consultative services as a therapist who can offer expressive arts therapies on a contracted basis and/or provide training to their school counselors/clinicians or teachers on the use and value of expressive arts therapies within pubic schools. Put together a packet of articles specializing in this area, as well as, a reading or resource list and send it to school principals, administrators, directors of guidance or clinical services with a well-thought-out proposal for how expressive arts therapies can benefit mainstream and "at-risk" children within public schools. Another person to contact is the director of the special education department and in addition to including the aforementioned materials, highlight how expressive arts therapies is an ideal modality in meeting a wide range of special needs in children.

Inclusion Programs

Many schools nationwide are instituting an inclusion model of education which require school systems to service children with a wide range of special needs. For years, this population of children have been successfully serviced by expressive arts therapies in specialized settings. This history would provide a natural link to continuing to service these children in their public school inclusion programs.

Developing After-Hours School-Based Expressive Arts Therapies Programs

Another way of working within a school system is to develop proposals for after-school, vacation and summer programs. These programs can offer a combination of creative, therapeutic, and educational activities which support the personal, academic, and social growth of children.

Importance of Professional Presentation

As someone interested in integrating expressive arts therapies into public schools, you are a pioneer and it is important to represent yourself and your profession impeccably. Be well-informed, articulate, clinically astute, and professional in your contact with school professionals. Provide them with information, publications, and research on how expressive arts therapies is a preferred treatment model in working with children. Through professional presentation we can demonstrate to others that much is to be gained by integrating expressive arts therapies into public schools.

Writing a Proposal to Promote the Addition of Expressive Arts Therapies Services to Schools and Other Settings

I.   Assessing the needs of the school or agency prior to writing proposal
- Population served
- Existing services
- Program philosophy
- Staffing
- Additional services needed, but not currently available

II.   Writing a proposal
- Statement of purpose
- Description of setting, population, program philosophy of school or agency, needs of agency
- Philosophy of expressive arts therapy
- Benefits of expressive arts therapy
- Work related responsibilities for an expressive arts therapist
- Proposed program description
- Program goals
- Variety of programming, sampling of groups
- Required materials, equipment, projected budget
- Space requirements for different modalities: adequate lighting, tables and chairs, sink, storage, wall surface or bulletin board, soundproofing, adequate space for movement, doors that close to create private space

III. Preparing a proposal packet
- Cover letter
- Proposal
- Resume
- Examples of groups
- Outline for in-service
- Articles, additional reading list

Developing a Format for Expressive Arts Therapies In-Service Presentation for Staff

I.   Describe overall program philosophy of clinical services for school or agency

II.   Introduce expressive arts therapy
- Brief historical and theoretical overview
- Unique advantages of expressive arts therapy

III. Experiential exercise for staff to further their understanding of expressive arts therapy

- Simple or novel media
- Relate exercise to specific group or population served by the agency
- Depending on size of staff, create an individual, dyad, or small group format

IV.   Slide presentation
- Slides/tapes/videos of work from current population (secure proper release forms)
- Slides/tapes/videos of work from other settings to illustrate new possibilities

V.   Hand-outs
- Relevant articles
- Protocols of current or proposed groups
- Current or proposed schedule of expressive arts therapy groups for the setting
- Additional reading list

Useful Questions to Ask at Informational or Site Interviews

The following list of questions can be helpful for expressive arts therapists inquiring about developing an expressive arts therapy program at a school site or for interns interviewing at potential training sites.

1. What is the past history and degree of reception of expressive arts therapy in the school?
2. What are their existing arts programs already in place: art, music, and drama? What is the potential for collaboration between the arts specialists and the expressive arts therapist or intern?
3. What is the availability and responsiveness of the on-site supervisor? What is his/her understanding of expressive arts therapy and its role within the school?
4. What are the expectations of parents, teachers, and counselors regarding expressive arts therapy in the school?
5. What are typical academic profiles and problems of the referred population: (a) learning disabilities; (b) ADHD; (c) bilingual speaking with English as a second language; (d) overachievement?
6. What is the school culture: socioeconomic, ethnic, and racial mix of students?
7. What are the numbers of: (a) bilingual families; (b) divorced families; (c) single parent families; (d) adoptions of older children; (e) children in foster care?
8. What different kinds of specialists are in the school currently serving special needs children? Are these credentialed professionals or stu-

dent interns from within specific disciplines?

9. What are typical home arrangements for students within the system of: (a) single family dwellings; (b) multiple family dwellings; (c) apartment living; (d) public housing or project living; (e) shelters?

10. What are the percentages for each district within the system of children bussed from different neighborhoods?

11. What are the kinds of family issues or problems that school-based counselors are most likely to encounter with the identified "at-risk" population: (a) violence; (b) abuse; (c) neglect; (d) truancy; (e) recently immigrant families; (f) alcohol and drug abuse; (g) poverty; (h) mental illness in the family?

12. What are some examples of typical school/family interventions made by counselors, principals, nurses, and teachers: (a) verbal counseling; (b) play therapy; (c) remedial academic tutoring; (d) probation and suspension; (e) medication?

13. What are some school-wide discipline policies? What are examples of incidents that typically result in suspension, and what are the terms of suspension?

14. Do you hold core evaluations or comparable meetings for children? Which children, how often, and who attends?

15. What is the kind of access to student's files, teacher reports, psychological testing outcomes, other kinds of test scores, and special needs services reports?

16. How would you describe the perceived strengths and weaknesses of this site?

Year in Review Program Evaluation

Whenever expressive arts therapies has been newly introduced to a school setting, it is important to review the program at the end of each year. It is recommended that all participants be encouraged to participate in a "year in review" meeting. These individuals should be involved in an evaluation process to determine the strengths and weaknesses of the year, and to develop new goals and strategies for the next year. The following form can assist participants to formulate their thoughts and ideas prior to the "year in review" meeting.

60   *Expressive Arts Therapies in Schools*

End-of-Year Program Review and Evaluation

Date:_____

Supervisor: _____

Supervisee: _____

Administrator: _____

1. Highlight the strengths of the training experience this year from your perspective.

2. Highlight the weaknesses of the training experience this year from your perspective.

3. Describe your experience of supervising or being supervised.

4. What recommendations you would like to make regarding supervision for next year?

5. Comment on your experience of collaborating with other professionals this year.

6. What are your recommendations for improving this program for next year?

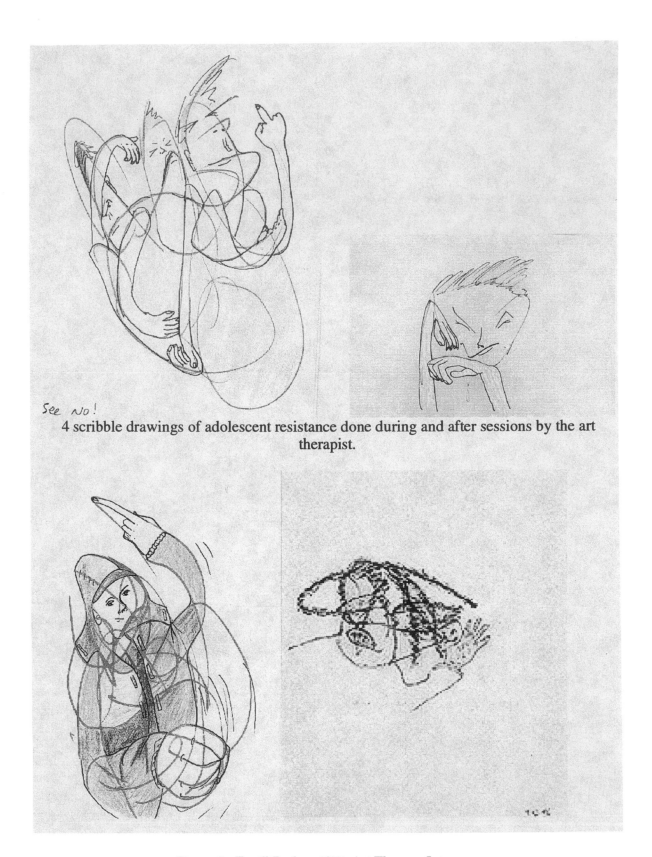

See No!

4 scribble drawings of adolescent resistance done during and after sessions by the art therapist.

Figure 8: Terrill Becker, 1977, Art Therapy Intern.

Chapter 8

CONCLUSION

Establishing expressive arts therapy programs in public schools is timely in its response to the inclusion model in education and to the increased presence of clinicians providing school-based mental health services to children and adolescents. According to a recent report in *Monitor*, the newsletter from the American Psychological Association (June 1997): "School-based health clinics have enjoyed explosive growth over the past several years, up 50% from two years before... The growth parallels an increased need for mental health services in schools as rising numbers of students struggle with family violence, substance abuse, and parental neglect."

Many of the school-based clinical services that are in place primarily provide screening, not treatment. Current clinical services along with some of the innovative social programming taking place in the classroom, remain tied to verbal modes of communication. There is a growing concern that "psychotherapies for children are often just 'junior' versions of the adult fare...Those techniques may lose their benefits in the translation from adult to child language. Many treatments that have proven successful for grown-ups may surpass a child's ability, or will, to comprehend...." (*Monitor*, June 1997, pp. 22).

In contrast, expressive arts therapy is a good developmental fit for children and adolescents, supporting normative patterns of communication through artistic expression. School-based expressive arts therapy programs promote a child's cognitive, emotional, and social development, contributing to improved academic performance. School-based expressive arts therapy programs service individual children and/or groups of children, while also enhancing school communities. School-based expressive arts therapy is becoming a treatment of choice and is meeting with increased receptivity across the country.

The Supervision and Program Development Guide, although designed ostensibly to establish an expressive arts therapy program within an educational system, can easily be adapted to establish a variety of alternative arts programming in nontraditional settings. The Supervision and Program Development Guide helps to conceptualize clear and "user-friendly" definitions, guidelines, and documentation. It informs administrators, educators, expressive arts therapists, supervisors, supervisees, and interns alike about the necessary steps to establish an effective arts program. The guide promotes conceptual thinking and the development of new program opportunities. It provides readers with a series of guidelines and program objectives in an effort to anticipate and problem-solve predictable, structural challenges in the initial phases of new programs.

In an era where funding is scarce and arts programming opportunities are limited, educators are called upon to support imaginative programming tools to expand educational horizons for students, universities, children, and communities. The Supervision and Program Development Guide is such a tool. This guide is intended to respond to the interests of both educators and expressive arts therapists struggling to serve the increasingly complex needs of both children and communities through the arts.

In *Schools of Hope*, Douglas H. Heath (1994) reiterates the necessity of a collaboration between schools and the community if we are to experience real change within our schools.

> To create schools of hope is not impossible. All it takes is a vision of human excellence, imagination, commitment, the will to persist—and a supportive community as well as responsive state and national governments. What other educational choice do we have, given the uncertain future for which we and our children must prepare ourselves? (Heath, 1994, p. 374.)

Expressive arts therapy has a role to play in creating "schools of hope." What has been outlined throughout this guide are suggestions and recommendations to take steps towards this goal. As in any new initiative, pioneers, visionaries, and foot soldiers are key players in bringing forward the changes and new forms which are surfacing throughout our schools nationwide. Expressive arts therapists are among this group with many more interested in joining. This guide will, hopefully, serve as a useful tool in the supervision and program development of expressive arts therapy.

Appendix A

CASE MANAGEMENT FORMS

INTERNSHIP AGREEMENT CONTRACT
(between college, site, and student)

_____This
is an agreement between _____(College) and
_____(Site) regarding the placement
of _____(Student)

The College agrees:

1. that the college will provide the site with written objectives and guidelines for the practicum/internship.

2. that the college supervisor will meet with the practicum/internship supervisor designated by the site's Program Director, a minimum of _____time(s) a semester to review the objectives and accomplishments of the student's practicum/internship and to evaluate his/her performance.

3. that the college supervisor will be available for consultation regarding any questions about the student's role or performance.

4. that the student show proof of a physical examination and a negative TB test to the practicum/internship site, prior to placement, if required by the practicum/internship site.

5. that the College would remove the student from the practicum/internship, if necessary, after mutual discussion between the Director of Field Training, practicum/internship supervisor, site supervisor, and student.

6. that each student shall be notified by the site of the student's obligation to observe all rules and regulations of the practicum/internship site, including those which pertain to the welfare and comfort of its clients. It is understood that the ultimate responsibility for the client is retained by the practicum/internship.

7. that the college will endeavor to include coverage for its students as additional insureds under its general liability policy for claims arising out of a bodily injury or property damage occurring while such students are acting under the supervision of _____ College, its servants, agents, or employees. Under no circumstances will the Institution, its servants, agents, or employees be deemed to be agents of the College.

The Institution agrees:

1. to accept _____, a student at _____College.

2. to designate an appropriate staff person to provide supervision and evaluation of the student's performance.

3. to inform the practicum/internship student about the operation of the program and acceptable behavior and practices expected of staff members.

4. to provide opportunities for practical and appropriate learning experiences for the practicum/internship student, which would include work with various participants of the program and activities, and attendance at appropriate meetings.

5. that the Institution would remove the student from the practicum/internship site, if necessary, after mutual discussion between practicum/internship supervisor, site supervisor,

and student.

6. that the student shall not be deemed an agent of _____College when performing services in the practicum/internship.

7. that the Institution will indemnify the College, its servants, agents, employees, and students against all claims arising out of acts or omissions occurring while students of the College are acting under the supervision, direction, or control of the Institution. The Institution will endeavor to include coverage under its professional liability insurance policy for students of _____ College when performing services in the practicum/internship sites.

8. The College may identify _____ (practicum or internship site) in its bulletins and publications as an institution that accepts college students for practicum/internships.

ADDENDUM: Expressive Arts Therapies Agreement

The Expressive Arts Therapies Program and the agency/school have agreed to the following additional guidelines:

1. The student will participate at this internship site for a minimum of _____ hours per week from _____ until _____ (dates).

2. Clinical responsibilities and the internship format are outlined on the attached **Internship Summary Sample** form and timeline. Approximately 60 percent of the intern's time should be devoted to direct clinical service.

3. **Supervision:**

   An Approved Supervisor site supervisor, with the appropriate credentials will meet with the student not less than one hour per week.

   a. An Approved Supervisor (by the College) will meet with the student for weekly supervision for a minimum of one hour.
   b. Whenever possible students should be supervised by Expressive Arts Therapists with appropriate registration.
   c. It is expected that supervision take place on a regular and consistent basis. The supervisor is responsible for assuring coverage for supervision in his/her absence.
   d. It is expected that the supervisor will serve as an advocate on behalf of the student within the Field Placement Site to ensure s/he receives an adequate orientation, caseload, space to see clients, supplies, basic art materials and equipment for expressive therapies interventions, access to files, access to group supervision or team meetings, if available, as well as, other training experiences.

4. The on-site supervisor will complete in-person and written evaluations of the student's performance as designated by the College.

5. If problems arise in regard to the student's performance on site, the following procedure should be observed:

   a. The student and site supervisor should discuss the problem.
   b. Initial contact should be made by the site supervisor to the campus *Expressive Arts Therapies Supervisor* (or vice versa).
   c. The campus supervisor will contact the College's Director of Field Training, or Program Director.

In the event that the student must be withdrawn, a written letter must be submitted to the college and signed by the clinical site supervisor and the student stating the reasons for the termination of the internship.

7. It is the expectation of the College that all organizations and individuals associated with its training program conduct their relationships with students in accordance with the ethical principles of the American Counseling Association and the American Psychological Association.

8. A copy of this agreement will become part of the student's permanent academic file.

This agreement shall commence on _____ and terminate on _____, unless the parties renew the agreement in writing, signed by all parties.

_____   _____
College Intern   Date

_____   _____
Site Supervisor   Date

_____   _____
College Administrator   Date

INTERNSHIP SUMMARY SHEET

Please **_print_** all information on this page.

Student: _____ Date: _____

Address: _____ City: _____

State: _____ ZIP: _____ Telephone: (_____)_____

Site: _____

Address: _____ City: _____

State: _____ ZIP: _____ Telephone: (_____)_____

Supervisor Name & Title: _____

Supervisor's Licensing/Certification Qualifications: _____

Learning Objectives: _____

_____

_____

_____

_____

_____

_____

_____

_____

Internship Responsibilities: Clinical Schedule / _Hourly_ Breakdown of Role:

_____

_____

_____

_____

_____

_____

_____

Total Hours/Week: _____ **Total Direct Client Contact Hours/Week:** _____

SAMPLE INTERNSHIP SUMMARY SHEET

Student: MARY SMITH   **Date:** 24 May 1997

Address: 1 Joy Street, Cambridge, MA 02138

Telephone: 617-868-8600 (home) 508-868-6900 (work)

Site: Top of The World School

Address: 7 Heaven Road, Boston, MA 02238

Telephone: 508-876-8900

(1) Supervisor Name and Title: Pam Blue, Art Therapist, School Counselor

Supervisor's Licensing/Certification Qualifications: M.A., A.T.R., L.M.H.C.

Beginning Date: 1 September 1997   **Ending Date:** 31 May 1998

Learning Objectives:

> Basic listening skills
>
> Interview and expressive arts therapies assessment techniques (including diagnosis)
>
> Ability to work with children and families
>
> Clear report writing
>
> Ability to use clinical/expressive arts therapies supervision appropriately
>
> Development of skills in confrontation and interpretation
>
> Expressive arts therapy group organization, work w/co-leader and therapy strategy
>
> Use of expressive arts therapy modalities in individual therapy sessions

Internship Responsibilities: Clinical Schedule/*Hourly* Breakdown of Role:

> 4 to 5 hours individual clients
>
> 5 hours of group counseling (includes planning)
>
> 2 hours intake
>
> 2 hours crisis intervention
>
> 1 hour individual supervision
>
> 2 hours group supervision
>
> 2 hours staff meetings/inservice training
>
> 2 hours administrative work

Total Hours/Week: 20–21 Total Direct Client Contact Hours/Week: 12–13

WEEKLY LOG

Week of: _____Arts/Expressive Therapy at:_____(School)

Expressive Arts Therapist/Supervisee:_____

INDIVIDUAL APPOINTMENTS

Student	Location	Day/Time	Comments

GROUP MEETINGS

Group/Co-leader	Location	Day/Time	Comments

SUPERVISION

Supervisor(s)	Location	Day/Time	Comments

PAPERWORK

Type	Day/Time	Comments

COMMUNICATION AND PLANNING

w/Professional (i.e. teacher, admin.)	Location	Day/Time	Comments

TEAM EVALUATION MEETINGS

Team	Location	Day/Time	Comments Related to Expressive Arts Treatment

IN-SERVICE TRAINING

Type of Training	Day/Time	Comments

REFERRAL FORM

Student's Name: _____ Male _____ Female _____

Age: _____ Grade: _____ Teacher's Name: _____

Date Referred: _____ For Individual: _____ Group _____

Short-term (4-8 weeks): _____ or Long-term (3-8 months): _____

Presenting problems:

Reason for referral:

Description of personality:

Overview of family history, cultural and socioeconomic background, home environment, family activities:

School history and academic performance:

After-school hours, structured or unstructured:

How does this student spend free time, personal interests, friendships:

Current support services, medications:

Short-term goals:

Long-term goals:

GROUP PROTOCOL FORM

Schedule

    Time:

    Location:

    Group Size:

    Co-leaders:

Group Description:

Goals:

Referral Criteria:

SAMPLE GROUP PROTOCOL FORM

Create a protocol that reflects the group's purpose, such as:

ADOLESCENT GIRL'S GROUP

Schedule

    Time:

    Location:

    Group Size:

    Co-Leaders: Art therapy student _____

                     Expressive therapy student _____

Group Description: An 8 week Group designed to explore a range of feelings self-concepts, relationships with peers, and school pressures. We will begin each session with a warm-up exercise, followed by a directed art experience that will serve to focus the group around a specific theme. Members will be encouraged to reflect upon and process their feelings together.

Goals: Improve communication skills, increase self-esteem, and promote self awareness through self-expression.

Referral Criteria:

    1. Females
    2. Ages 12-14
    3. Must be able to make an 8 week commitment
    4. An interest in the arts or a willingness to use art as a vehicle of expression

MINI-CASE STUDY PRESENTATION FORM

Student's Name: _____ Male _____ Female _____

Age: _____ Grade: _____ Teacher's Name: _____

Date Referred: _____ For Individual: _____ or Group _____

Short-term (4-8 weeks): _____ or Long-term (3-8 months): _____

Brief overview of family history:

Brief overview of school functioning and performance:

Reason for referral to expressive arts therapy:

Recommended goals for treatment:

Describe the session: task presented, materials, art process, time frame, group or individual work:

Describe imagery: developmental and dynamic assessment:

Comments on the child's attitude toward the task:

Describe the child's relationship with you:

Ideas for continued work:

Questions:

THESAURUS FOR PROCESS NOTES:
ART, MOVEMENT, MUSIC

The thesaurus was added to help supervisees translate the expressive art therapy they do into a written format. It is presented as a beginning, to help familiarize supervisees the language of documentation. As they grow in their clinical work, this vocabulary will increase. A thesaurus format can be adopted to create a process note specific to each modality.

Thesaurus Specific to the Arts Modalities

ART

barriers	line quality	transparency	scribbling	use of space
disorganized	color	underlining	cartooning	
shading	form	omissions	tadpoles	
reversals	erasures	perspective	x-ray	

MOVEMENT

bound/flow	use of far reach space	use of near reach
shape/flow	rigid	widened/narrowed
fluid	sustained	breath awareness
quick	demonstrates body/mind connection	
direct	can lead and follow	facilitates movement
enveloping	dynamic	stereotypical

MUSIC

matches pitch	demonstrates musical co-activity
sings songs	demonstrates musical creativity
sings phrases in tonality	sustains musical activity
imitates rhythmic patterns	uses voice expressively
initiates rhythmic patterns	responds to changes in dynamics
imitates melodic phrases	responds to changes in tempo
initiates melodic phrases	demonstrates self expressive musical confidence
demonstrates evoked musical responses	

ART THERAPY PROCESS NOTE

Client:

Date:

Session #:

I. THEME / DIRECTIVE /PROCEDURE

(Include instructions given, tasks, or techniques explained.)

II. APPROACH TO TASK / MATERIALS

___ organized	___ impulsive	___ follows directions
___ disorganized	___ thoughtful	___ doesn't follow directions
___ distracted	___ constricted	___ able to problem-solve
___ concentrated	___ spontaneous	___ poor frustration tolerance

(Verbal associations, descriptions)

III. ATTITUDE / BEHAVIOR

___ motivated	___ restless	___ compliant
___ reluctant	___ oppositional	___ initiates
___ withdrawn	___ focused	___ demanding
___ disruptive	___ confident	___ cooperative
___ intrusive	___ inhibited	___ aggressive
___ passive	___ controlled	___ enthusiastic
___ assertive	___ anxious	

(Verbalizations)

III. IMAGERY

___ empty

___ integrated

___ abstract

___ representational

___ creative

___ stereotypical

___ encapsulated

___ lacks boundaries

STYLE

___ detailed

___ chaotic

___ fluid

___ fragmented

___ cohesive

___ tentative

___ dynamic

___ pressured

EXPRESSION

___ expansive

___ constricted

___ impulsive

___ controlled

___ spontaneous

___ rigid

___ explorative

___ perfectionistic

(Describe sequence; work completed; work destroyed)

IV. AFFECT

___ anxiety confusion   ___ anxious   ___ confused   ___ tearful

___ anger   ___ constricted   ___ indifference

(Describe verbalizations, body language, coping mechanisms)

V. THERAPIST'S REACTIONS

___ anxiety   ___ concern   ___ confusion

___ frustration   ___ sympathy   ___ dislike

___ satisfaction   ___ anger   ___ intimidation

___ sadness   ___ overwhelm

(Describe reactions, include possible countertransferential themes)

VI. INTERACTIONS WITH PEERS IN GROUP

___ relates well   ___ dominates   ___ competitive   ___ friendly

___ helpful   ___ isolated   ___ passive   ___ antagonistic

___ dependent   ___ playful   ___ oppositional   ___ manipulative

(Describe interactions, verbal and nonverbal)

VII. RELATIONSHIP TO GROUP LEADER

___ dependent   ___ eager to please   ___ sneaky   ___ polite

___ resistant   ___ inappropriate   ___ guarded   ___ hostile

___ friendly   ___ remote   ___ trusting   ___ challenging

___ compliant   ___ suspicious   ___ responsive   ___ withholding

(Describe relationship, overt and covert agendas)

VIII. TRANSITIONS TO AND FROM GROUP

___smooth   ___disorganized   ___ tantrums   ___regresses

___rocky   ___settles quickly   ___anticipates   ___ uneven

___oriented to schedule

(Describe transition patterns)

IX. GOALS

___ improve self-esteem through mastery

___ improve task skills (concentration, problem solving, etc.)

___ improve interpersonal and communication skills

___ improve self-control through release of tension

___ increase risk taking, creative expression, and spontaneity

___ increase self-awareness and integration of experience

(Address strengths and weaknesses; defenses; developmental levels)

X. PLANS

(Ideas for next session.)

EXPRESSIVE ARTS THERAPIES CONSENT FORM

Consent to Use and Display
ARTISTIC PRODUCTS

I, _____, give permission to _____ to use and /or display art, dance, or music pieces created by me in a professional setting for the purpose of supervision or education on the therapeutic use of art, dance, or music therapy. It is my understanding that my name will not be revealed in any presentation or display of my artistic work.

This consent to disclose may be revoked by me at any time except to the extent that action has been taken in reliance thereon.

Patient/Client _____   Date _____

Witness _____   Date _____

PERMISSION TO AUDIOTAPE/VIDEOTAPE FORM

DATE: _____

Recording of Interviews

I give my permission to _____ to record on:

❏ Audiotape

❏ Videotape

my participation in _____ (specific nature of taping).

I have been informed that all information recorded will be held in strictest confidence and that the recordings are solely for the purposes of clinical treatment, teaching and supervision. In order to ensure confidentiality, these tapes will be retained in the safe possession of the interviewer until erased. Access to them will be strictly limited to the above-mentioned purposes. All recorded information will be erased upon the termination of treatment.

SIGNED _____

WITNESS _____

RELATIONSHIP _____

TERMINATION REPORT

Client:_____

Therapist:_____ Date:_____

Identifying Information:

> age/ sex/ ethnicity
>
> diagnosis
>
> family demographics
>
> previous treatment
>
> medications
>
> reasons for referral
>
> presenting concerns

Course of Treatment:

> length of treatment
>
> treatment setting (individual/ dyad/ group)
>
> description of behavioral difficulties over time
>
> use of and reaction to expressive arts therapy
>
> significant changes in:
>
>> behavior
>>
>> family
>>
>> medication
>>
>> environment
>>
>> school performance
>>
>> insight into difficulties
>>
>> peer relationships
>>
>> clinical formulation

Conclusion and Goals:

strengths

areas of continued difficulties

goals achieved

recommendations for future treatment

_____

Therapist's Signature

Appendix B

EVALUATION FORMS

EVALUATION OF CLINICAL SKILLS

Supervisee: _____	**Date:** _____
Site: _____	
Supervisor: _____	

I. Clinical and Professional Functioning

Assessment and Evaluation Skills

Overall Rating _____

_____ Level of understanding client problems

_____ Effective history-taking and background information

_____ Ability to identify client interpersonal relationship patterns

_____ Clear and concise presentation in supervision or diagnostic meetings

_____ Ability to recommend appropriate treatment or referral

Comments:

Counseling Skills

Overall Rating _____

_____ Ability to do initial assessment and differential diagnosis on a continuum of health and pathology

_____ Level of verbal and nonverbal listening and observation skills

_____ Level of diagnostic skills and ability to provide a five-axis DSM IV diagnosis

_____ Ability to contexualize socioeconomic, political, cultural, racial and gender-based issues

_____ Ability to conceptualize the effect of developmental factors in client cases

_____ Ability to translate conceptualization of counseling cases and theoretical understanding into appropriate treatment interventions

_____ Level of understanding of the impact of the socioeconomic, political, cultural, racial and gender-based aspects on the world view of the counselor and the client

_____ Effectively maintains a multicultural perspective in working with culturally diverse populations.

_____ Level of clinical writing skills: ability to write progress and process notes, intake forms, and termination summaries

_____ Level of presentation skills: ability to present a clear and concise case conference material

Comments:

Therapeutic Relationship with Clients

Overall Rating _____

_____ Quality of therapeutic rapport established with clients

_____ Ability to empathize with clients and reflect the feelings the client is conveying

_____ Effectively encourages client participation in the therapeutic process

_____ Utilizes culturally appropriate verbal and nonverbal communication with clients

_____ Effectively sets clear goals with clients that shape the counseling process

_____ Ability to set clear, supportive limits and follow through on limit setting

_____ Effectively responds to client resistance, fear and ambivalence

_____ Ability to clarify with client when there are inconsistencies or discrepancies in behavior or relaying of information

_____ Effectively identifies relational issues such as transference and countertransference

_____ Ability to terminate effectively

Comments:

Group Skills (if applicable)

Overall Rating _____

_____   Knowledge of group theory and background

_____   Knowledge of how groups develop dynamically

_____   Development of a conceptual framework for understanding group process

_____   Awareness of appropriate interventions in group process

____   Ability to appreciate and handle both the task and maintenance aspects of group leadership

_____   Ability to run both therapeutic and nontherapeutic (task, work) groups effectively

_____   Level of competence in co-leadership skills

Comments:

Counselor Identify Development

Overall Rating _____

_____   Demonstrates knowledge of federal and state laws and regulations affecting counseling

_____   Demonstrates knowledge of local, state and federal referral agencies and procedures

_____   Demonstrates knowledge of the ACA Code of Ethics and Standards of Practice

_____   Conducts himself/herself in an ethical manner

Comments:

Professional Skills

Overall Rating _____

_____ Understanding of the site as a political, social, economic and cultural system

_____ Effectively communicates with colleagues and outside professionals

_____ Ability to collaborate as a member of an interdisciplinary team

_____ Ability to provide consultation services

_____ Effectively identifies, utilizes and develops community resources

_____ Performance in administrative and staff meetings

_____ Level of accountability and dependability

_____ Takes initiative and follows through on tasks

_____ Demonstrates resourcefulness and flexibility

_____ Ability to use feedback constructively

_____ Ability to give feedback constructively

Comments:

Self-Awareness Skills

Overall Rating _____

_____ Level of emotional adjustment and maturity

_____ Level of self-awareness, self-knowledge

_____ Understanding of self in relationship to issues of race, gender, ethnicity, age, class, sexual orientation and religion

Comments:

II. Use of Supervision

_____ Actively participates in self-critique and evaluation

_____ Awareness of own dynamics in relationship

_____ Uses self-disclosure appropriately in supervision

_____ Openness to learn from supervisor

_____ Prepares for supervision

_____ Ability to accept and utilize feedback provided by supervisor

_____ Ability to share and learn from colleagues in group supervision (if applicable)

Comments:

Areas of Strength and Further Development

In the space below provide the supervisee with feedback concerning his or her strengths and recommendations for further development in clinical and other professional areas.

Strengths:

Areas for Further Development:

I have read and discussed this evaluation with my supervisor:

_____   _____

Supervisee's signature   Supervisor's signature

EVALUATION OF ART THERAPY SKILLS

Supervisee: _____	**Date:** _____
Site: _____	
Supervisor: _____	

This form reviews areas of evaluation for art therapy skills. Rate the supervisee's level of performance or improvement in each of the categories listed below by using the 5 point rating scale. Space has been left at the end of each section for additional comments.

Ratings: **1 - Unsatisfactory**   **2 - Satisfactory with Concerns**   **3 - Good**

            4 - Very Good   **5 - Outstanding**   **or**   **N/A** (not applicable)

_____ Ability to understand the art therapy process

_____ Able to assess clients through art

_____ Skillful at observing the client's process and artworks

_____ Ability to plan and execute an art/expressive arts therapies warm-up exercise and execute closure

_____ Understands and articulates rationale for use of art in therapy

_____ Knowledge of arts materials and use of materials to fosters client's creativity

_____ Uses art along with verbalization to heighten client's awareness and foster therapeutic change

_____ Able to provide technical assistance with the art media

_____ Uses and cares for client art products professionally (i.e., appropriate storage of artwork, use of releases)

_____ Uses directives flexibly

_____ Ability to apply different theoretical approaches of art therapy

_____ Ability to develop art therapy treatment goals for groups and individuals and to apply them with clients

_____ Has knowledge of group dynamics, specifically the formative stages of groups, and structuring art therapy sessions for groups

_____ Ability to maintain identity as an art therapist while functioning as a team member

_____ Ability to write progress notes and art therapy documentation as required by site

_____ Knows and follows AATA Code of Ethics

Additional Comments on Art/Expressive Arts Therapies Skills:

I have read and discussed this evaluation with my supervisor:

_____   _____
          Supervisee's signature   Supervisor's signature

EVALUATION OF DANCE THERAPY SKILLS

Supervisee: _____	**Date:** _____
Site: _____	
Supervisor: _____	

This form reviews areas of evaluation for dance therapy skills. Rate the supervisee's level of performance or improvement in each of the categories listed below by using the 5 point rating scale. Space has been left at the end of each section for additional comments.

Ratings: **1 - Unsatisfactory**   **2 - Satisfactory with Concerns**   **3 - Good**

4 - Very Good   **5 - Outstanding or   N/A** (not applicable)

_____ Ability to understand the dance therapy process

_____ Ability to assess through movement

_____ Ability to plan and execute a movement warm-up; develop movement; and execute movement closure

_____ Understands and articulates rationale for use of dance in therapy

_____ Ability to notice clients' movement cues

_____ Ability to reflect on own movement style

_____ Uses directives flexibly

_____ Uses and cares for client products professionally (i.e., appropriate use of releases for videos)

_____ Ability to apply different theoretical approaches of dance therapy

_____ Ability to develop dance therapy treatment goals for groups and individuals and to apply them with clients

_____ Has knowledge of group dynamics, specifically the formative stages of groups, and structuring dance therapy sessions for groups

_____ Ability to maintain identity as a dance therapist while functioning as a team member

_____ Ability to write progress notes and dance therapy documentation as required by site

_____ Knows and follows ADTA Code of Ethics

Additional Comments on Dance/Expressive Arts Therapies Skills:

I have read and discussed this evaluation with my supervisor:

_____   _____

      Supervisee's signature   Supervisor's signature

EVALUATION OF MUSIC THERAPY SKILLS

Supervisee: _____ **Date:** _____

Site: _____

Supervisor: _____

This form reviews areas of evaluation for music therapy skills. Rate the supervisee's level of performance or improvement in each of the categories listed below by using the 5 point rating scale. Space has been left at the end of each section for additional comments.

Ratings: **1 - Unsatisfactory**   **2 - Satisfactory with Concerns**   **3 - Good**

           4 - Very Good   **5 - Outstanding**   **or**   **N/A** (not applicable)

_____ Ability to understand the music therapy process

_____ Ability to assess through music

_____ Ability to plan and execute a music/expressive arts therapies warm-up exercise and execute closure

_____ Formulates music therapy strategies to achieve goals

_____ Uses music along with verbalization to heighten client's awareness and foster therapeutic change

_____ Demonstrates understanding of improvisational techniques for use of music in therapy

_____ Understands and articulates rationale for use of music in therapy

_____ Uses directives flexibly

_____ Ability to apply different theoretical approaches of music therapy

_____ Uses and cares for client products professionally (i.e., appropriate use of releases for recording)

_____ Ability to develop music therapy treatment goals for groups and individuals and to apply them with clients

_____ Has knowledge of group dynamics, specifically the formative stages of groups, and structuring music therapy sessions for groups

_____ Ability to maintain identity as a music therapist while functioning as a team member

_____   Ability to write progress notes and music therapy documentation as required by site

_____   Knows and follows AMTA Code of Ethics

Additional Comments on Music/Expressive Arts Therapies Skills:

I have read and discussed this evaluation with my supervisor:

_____   _____
Supervisee's signature   Supervisor's signature

EVALUATION OF EXPRESSIVE ARTS THERAPIES SKILLS

Supervisee: _____ **Date:** _____

Site: _____

Supervisor: _____

This form reviews areas of evaluation for expressive arts therapies skills. Rate the supervisee's level of performance or improvement in each of the categories listed below by using the 5 point rating scale. Space has been left at the end of each section for additional comments.

Ratings: 1 - Unsatisfactory   2 - Satisfactory with Concerns   3 - Good
4 - Very Good   5 - Outstanding   or   N/A (not applicable)

_____ Able to assess clients through expressive modalities

_____ Skillful at observing the client's process and expressive works

_____ Ability to plan and execute an expressive arts therapies warm-up exercise and execute closure

_____ Understands and articulates rationale for use of expressive modalities in therapy

_____ Uses expressive arts therapies with verbalization to heighten client's awareness and foster therapeutic change

_____ Knowledge of when to shift modalities to further the therapeutic process (intermodal transfer)

_____ Knowledge of expressive materials and use of materials to foster client's creativity

_____ Uses and cares for client expressive products professionally (i.e., appropriate storage of products, use of releases)

_____ Uses directives flexibly

_____ Ability to apply different theoretical approaches of expressive arts therapies

_____ Ability to develop expressive arts therapy treatment goals for groups and individuals and to apply them with clients

_____ Has knowledge of group dynamics, specifically the formative stages of groups, and structuring expressive arts therapy sessions for groups

_____ Ability to maintain identity as an expressive arts therapist while functioning as a team member

_____ Ability to write progress notes and expressive arts therapy documentation as required by site

Additional Comments on Expressive Arts Therapies Skills:

I have read and discussed this evaluation with my supervisor:

_____   _____

Supervisee's signature   Supervisor's signature

Appendix C

ADDITIONAL RESOURCES

NATIONAL EXPRESSIVE ARTS THERAPIES ORGANIZATIONS

American Art Therapy Association (AATA)
1202 Allanson Road
Mundelein, IL 60060
(847) 949-6064
E-mail: arttherapy@ntr.net
http://www.arttherapy.org

American Dance Therapy Association (ADTA)
2000 Century Plaza, Suite 108
Columbia, MD 21044-3263
(410) 997-4040
E-mail: info@adta.org
http://www.adta.org

National Coalition of Arts Therapies (NCATA)
2117 L Street, N.W. #274
Washington, D.C. 20037
(202)678-6787
http://ncatacom/

American Music Therapy Association (AMTA)
8455 Colesville Road Suite 1000
Silver Spring, MD 20910
(301) 589-3300
E-mail: info@musictherapy.org
http://www.namt.org

American Association for Music Therapy (AAMT)
1 Station Plaza
Ossining, N.Y. 10562
(914) 944-9260

National Association for Poetry Therapy (NAPT)
P.O. Box 551
Port Washington, N.Y. 11050
(516) 944-9791
E-mail: aseeger@mcimail.com
http://www.poetrytherapy.org

National Association for Drama Therapy (NADT)
15245 Shady Grove Road
Suite 130
Rockville, MD 20850
(301) 258-9210
E-mail: nadt@danielgroup.com
http://www.NADT.org

American Society of Group Psychotherapy and Psychodrama
E-mail: edgarcia@artswire.org.
http://www.artswire.org

Expressive Therapy Concepts Referral Bank
http://expressivetherapy.org/refbank.html

NATIONAL COUNSELING ASSOCIATIONS

American Counseling Association (ACA)
5999 Stevenson Ave.
Alexandria, VA 22304
Tele: (703) 823-9800
E-mail: webmaster@counseling.org
http://www.counseling.org/

American Mental Health Counselor's Association (AMHCA)
P.O. Box 79207
Baltimore, MD 21279-0207
Tele: (800) 326-2642

RECOMMENDED READINGS

Allan, J., & Berry, P. (1987). Sandplay *Elementary School Guidance and Counseling, 21,* pp. 300-306.

Anmann, R. (1991). *Healing and Transformation in Sandplay.* Chicago: Open Court.

Bush, J. (1997). *The Handbook of School Art Therapy.* Springfield, IL: Charles C Thomas Publisher, Ltd.

Butler, K. (1997). The Anatomy of Resilience. *The Family Therapy Networker,* March/April 1997, pp. 22-31.

Campbell, D. (1989). *The Roar of Silence: Healing Powers of Breath, Tone And Music.* London: Quest Books.

Campenelli, M. (1990). Dialogue letter writing. *Art Therapy, 7,* pp. 42-43.

Carey, L. (1990). Sandplay therapy with a troubled child. *Arts in Psychotherapy, 18,* pp. 231-239.

Carmichael, K. D. (1994). Sandplay as an elementary school strategy. *Elementary School Guidance and Counseling, 28,* pp. 302-307.

Case, C., & Dalley, T. (1990). Images and integration: Art therapy in a multi-cultural school. *Working with Children in Art.* London: Tavistock/Routledge.

Cassity, M. D., & Cassity, J. E. (1995). *Multimodal Psychiatric Music Therapy.* St. Louis, MO: MMB Music Inc.

Cattanach, A. (1995). Psychodrama and play therapy with young children. *Arts in Psychotherapy, 22,* pp. 223-228.

Dieckmann, H. (1986). *Twice Told Tales: The Psychological Use of Fairy Tales.* Wilmette, IL: Chiron Publications.

Essex, M., Frostig., K., & Hertz, J. (1996). In the service of children: Art and expressive therapies in public schools. *American Journal of Art Therapy, 13,* pp. 181-190.

Edwards, D. (1993). Learning about feelings: The role of supervision in art therapy training. *Arts in Psychotherapy, 20,* pp. 213-222.

Forsyth, P. & Tallerico, M. (1993). Understanding the urban context and condition of practice of school administration. *City Schools.* California: Corwin Press, Inc.

Franklin, M. (1990). The esthetic attitude and empathy: A point of convergence. *American Journal of Art Therapy, 29,* pp. 42-47.

Gersie, A. (1995). Arts therapies practice in inner-city slums: Beyond the installation of hope. *Arts in Psychotherapy, 22,* pp. 207-215.

Goleman, D., (1995). *Emotional Intelligence.* New York: Bantam Books, pp. 231-287.

Gordon, D. (1978). *Therapeutic Metaphors.* Cupertino, CA: Meta Publications.

Graham, J. (1994). The art of emotionally disturbed adolescents: Designing a drawing program to address violent imagery. *American Journal of Art Therapy, 32,* pp. 115-121.

Heath, D. Creating schools of hope: Seven essential steps. *Schools of Hope.* San Francisco: Jossey-Bass Publishers.

Heninger, O. E. (1981). *American Guide of Psychiatry.* S. Arieti & H. K. H. Brodie. Volume 7, pp. 553-563.

Herrmann, U. (1995). A Trojan house of clay: Art therapy in a residential school for the blind. *Arts in Psychotherapy, 22,* pp. 229-234.

Hynes, A. M., & Hynes-Berry, M. (1986). *Bibliotherapy—The Interactive Process: A Guide.* Boulder & London: Westview Press.

James, B. (1989). *Treating Traumatized Children.* Lexington, MA: Lexington Books.

James, R., & Vinturella, L. (1987). Sandplay: A therapeutic medium with children. *Elementary School Guidance and Counseling, 21,* pp. 229-238.

Jung, C. G. (1961). *Memories, Dreams, Reflections.* New York: Vintage Books.

Hobbs, B., & Collison, B. (1995). School-community agency collaboration: Implications for the school counselor. *The School Counselor, 43,* pp., 58-65.

Kramer, E. (1971). *Art as Therapy with Children.* New York: Stockmen Books.

Knuckle-Miller, C. (1990). Potentials and problems in establishing an art therapy program in a residential school for children who are deaf. *American Journal of Art Therapy, 29,* pp. 34-41.

Landgarten H. (1981). *Clinical Art Therapy.* New York: Brunner/Mazel.

Leedy, J. (1985). *Poetry as Healer.* New York: Vanguard Press.

Lerner, A. (1983). *Words For All Seasons.* Northridge, CA: Being Books.

Lerner, A. (1982). Poetry therapy in the group experience. *In:* Abt, L.E. & Stuart, I.R. (Eds.) *The Newer Therapies: A Sourcebook.* pp. 228-247. New York: Van Nostrand Reinhold Company.

Linesch, D. (1988). *Adolescent Art Therapy.* New York: Brunner / Mazel, Inc.

Lowenfeld, V., & Brittain, W. (1987). *Creative and Mental Growth.* Eighth Ed. New York: Macmillan Co.

Malchiodi, C. (1990). *Breaking the Silence: Art Therapy.* New York: Brunner / Mazel, Inc.

Malchiodi, C., & Riley, S. (1996). *Supervision and Related Issues: A Handbook for Professionals.* Chicago, IL: Magnolia Street Publishers.

Malchiodi, C. (1997). Editorial: Art therapy in schools. *American Journal of Art Therapy, 14,* pp. 2-4.

Nachmanovitch, S. (1990). *Free Play: The Power of Improvisation in Life and the Arts.* Los Angeles: Jeremy Tarcher Inc.

Thomas, C. C., & Osna-Heller, P. (1987). Reflections: The three pillars of biblio/poetry Therapy. *Arts in Psychotherapy, 14,* pp. 341-344.

Packard, S., & Anderson, F. (1976). A shared identity crisis: Art education and art therapy. *Art Therapy, 16,* pp. 21-28.

Riley, S. (1992). Supervision and the issue of case management. *Art Therapy, 16,* pp. 21-28

Riordan, R. (1996). Scriptotherapy: Therapeutic writing as a counseling adjunct. *Journal of Counseling and Development, 74,* pp. 263-269.

Robbins, A. (1994). *Becoming an Art Therapist: A Multi-Modal Approach to Creative Art Therapy.* London: Jessica Kingsley Publishers, Ltd.

Rubin, J. (1984). Understanding and helping children grow through art. *Child Art Therapy.* New York: Van Nostrand Reinhold.

Rubin, R. J. (1978). *Using Bibliotherapy: A Guide to Theory and Practice.* Phoenix: Oryx Press.

Sleek, S. (1997). School-based health care is gaining in popularity. *Monitor, American Psychological Association,* June 1997.

Spaniol, S. (1990). *Organizing Exhibitions of Art By People With Mental Illness: A Step-By-Step Manual.* Boston: Center for Psychiatric Rehabilitation, Boston University.

Steinhardt, L. (1993). Children in art therapy as abstract expressionist painters. *American Journal of Art Therapy, 31,* pp. 113-120.

Ulman, E., & Dachinger, P. (1975). *Art Therapy In Theory and Practice.* New York: Schoken Books.

Wadeson, H. (1987). *The Dynamics of Art Psychotherapy.* New York: John Wiley and Sons.

Wadeson, H. (1993). The active muse. *Arts in Psychotherapy, 20,* pp 173-184.

Weinrib, E. L. (1983). *Images of the Self.* Boston: Sigo Press.

Williams, A. (1989). *The Passionate Technique: Strategic Psychodrama With Individuals, Families and Groups*. Tavistock, London.

Zeiger, R. (1994). Use of the journal in treatment of the seriously disturbed adolescent: A case study. *Arts in Psychotherapy, 21,* pp. 197-204.

Zuckerman, E. L. (1995). *Clinician's Thesaurus*. New York: The Guilford Press.